Blue Ribbon Cookies

Pictured on the cover:
Acorns, p. 7; Viennese Walnut Cookies, p. 15;
Kifli, p. 16; Apricot Blossoms, p. 91;
Butterhorns, p. 3

Blue Ribbon Cookies

A Country Kitchens Press book
P.O. Box 7453
University Station
Provo, Utah 84602

Distributed by:

Follett Publishing Company
1010 West Washington Boulevard
Chicago, Illinois 60607

Cover design & layout: Carole Wade

Photography: Borge B. Anderson & Associates

ISBN No. 0-9601656-2-2

First Printing 1978

The Best Cookies – from the Best Cooks!

The **Blue Ribbon Cookies** book features some of the best cookies in America from some of the best cooks in America — the Blue Ribbon winners from the State and County Fairs.

No other baking contest is as competitive as the cookie contest since *everyone* makes cookies. That coveted prize, the Blue Ribbon, really means something in the cookie division! And, some of the cookies were good enough to also merit awards of $100, and one cookie was even awarded $1,000.00 by a national cookie company!

There are lunch box cookies that will bring requests for repeats, make-ahead refrigerator cookies, holiday and special occasion treats, nationality favorites from other lands, and, rich and delicious dessert cookies. No matter what kind of cookie you crave, you'll find a prize-winning version in the **Blue Ribbon Cookies** book.

You'll also make the best brownies in town. And, if you want to establish a reputation as a great cookie chef, then try serving the *California Cream Cheese Cookies,* the *Luscious Lemon Bars,* or the favorite in our test kitchen, *Fudge Nut Bars.*

All the cookies in the **Blue Ribbon Cookies** book are simply special — even the old-fashioned sugar cookies have a special "Old-World Bake Shoppe" flavor you'll love!

Contents

Special occasion cookies

Butterscotch Lace Cookies

Very pretty party fare and sure to be a conversation piece. While baking, the dough separates into very fragile lace-like designs.

1 cup butter, melted
1½ cups brown sugar
1½ cups quick rolled oats
1 cup fine unsweetened coconut (nutrition store)
1 egg, slightly beaten
1 teaspoon vanilla
4 tablespoons flour
¼ teaspoon salt

Combine butter, brown sugar, rolled oats and coconut; let stand at room temperature overnight.

Add remaining ingredients to oat mixture. Drop by level teaspoonful 3″ apart on well-buttered cookie sheet; press to flatten slightly. Bake only 6 or 9 cookies at a time.

Bake at 350° for 5 to 7 minutes or until golden brown. Watch carefully. Cool 2 minutes before removing to paper towel covered rack. Makes 6 dozen.

Note: Lace cookies will absorb moisture in humid weather and become limp. Immediately store between wax paper in air tight tin.

For party fare, brush bottoms of cooled cookies with melted chocolate chips. Place upside down on wax paper until chocolate sets.

Marilyn Martell
Robert Martell
Thousand Oaks, California

Marilyn Martell, *County Fair Prize Cookies*, Prize Publishers, P. O. Box 281, Port Hueneme, California. Used by permission of Prize Publishers.

Pineapple Party Cookies

(photo on page 56)

Beautiful! A tangy golden pineapple filling peeks through tiny designs cut in the top of the cookie. You can reflect the holiday season or special occasion by the design you select.

½ cup shortening
1 cup sugar
2 eggs
1 teaspoon vanilla
2½ cups flour, sifted
¼ teaspoon soda
½ teaspoon salt

Cream shortening, sugar and eggs thoroughly. Mix in vanilla.

Sift dry ingredients together. Add to creamed mixture, blending well. Chill dough.

Roll dough 1/16-inch thick on floured board. Cut with round cutter or any desired shape about 2½ inches in diameter, cutting 2 alike for each cookie. For a decorative effect, cut the center out of the top cookie with a tiny heart, star or scalloped cutter.

Place the bottom pieces on lightly greased baking sheet. Spread a rounded teaspoonful of cooled filling on each. Cover with top cookie. Press edges together with floured tines of fork or fingertips.

Bake at 400° for 8 to 10 minutes or until delicately browned. Makes 4½ dozen.

Tangy Pineapple Filling

1 cup sugar
¼ cup flour
1½ cups crushed pineapple, well drained
¼ cup lemon juice
3 tablespoons butter
¼ teaspoon nutmeg
¾ cup pineapple juice

Blend sugar and flour in saucepan. Stir in remaining ingredients. Cook slowly, stirring constantly, until thickened (5 to 10 minutes). Cool. Makes 2-2/3 cups filling.

Storme H. Rose
Colorado Springs, Colorado

Butterhorns

(photo on cover)

Delicate and delicious sour cream pastries with a spicy nut filling – yummy!

Pastry:
1 cup butter, softened
¾ cup sour cream
1 egg yolk
2 cups flour

Filling:
2 teaspoons cinnamon
¾ cup sugar
1 cup finely chopped walnuts or pecans

Blend softened butter with sour cream. Add egg yolk and mix well. Blend in flour (dough will be sticky). Separate into 3 balls. Wrap and refrigerate overnight.

Remove dough from refrigerator, let stand a short time. Roll on well-floured surface into circle approximately 16 inches in diameter. Cut into quarters. Sprinkle each quarter with filling mixture. Cut each quarter into fourths. Roll from wide end to narrow end, shaping into butterhorn.

Place on greased cookie sheets.

Bake at 350° for 30 to 35 minutes.

Reneé Herman
Albuquerque, New Mexico

Schaum Tortes

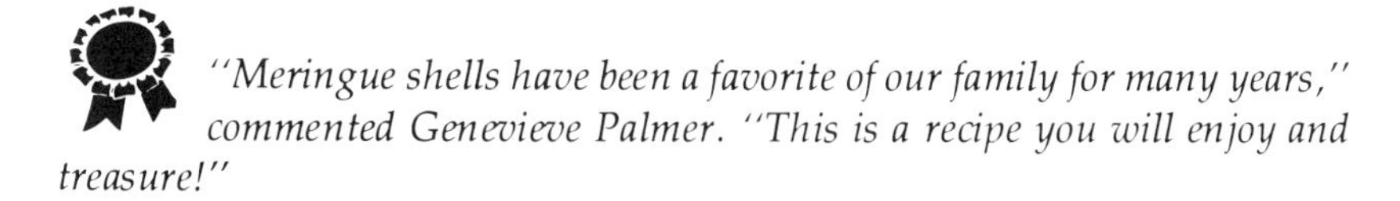

"Meringue shells have been a favorite of our family for many years," commented Genevieve Palmer. "This is a recipe you will enjoy and treasure!"

6 egg whites
¼ teaspoon cream of tartar
2 cups sugar
1 tablespoon white vinegar
1 teaspoon vanilla

Beat egg whites until foamy. Add cream of tartar and sugar gradually; beat until stiff peaks form. Add vinegar and vanilla; beat until well-blended.

Drop by rounded teaspoons onto a greased cookie sheet.

Bake at 275° for 45 to 60 minutes until firm but not brown. Serve with fresh fruit and whipped cream.

Genevieve Palmer
Salt Lake City, Utah

Petite Lemon Tarts

(photo on page 56)

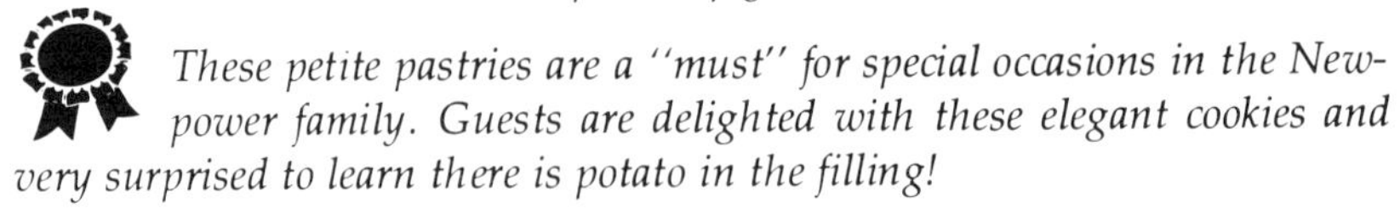

These petite pastries are a "must" for special occasions in the Newpower family. Guests are delighted with these elegant cookies and very surprised to learn there is potato in the filling!

1 cup flour
2 tablespoons sugar
½ cup butter
2 tablespoons milk

Sift flour and sugar together. Cut in butter. Stir in milk.

Pat small amounts of dough into tiny muffin or tart tins. Chill while preparing filling.

Fill tart shells with Tangy Lemon Filling; place on cookie sheet.

Bake at 300° for 8 minutes then increase temperature to 375° and continue baking until edges are browned lightly. The tarts can be glazed with a thin powdered sugar frosting while hot, if desired.

Tangy Lemon Filling

⅝ cup sugar
1 tablespoon butter, melted
1 egg
1 medium potato, cooked and grated
Grated rind of 1 lemon
2 - 3 tablespoons lemon juice

Combine sugar and melted butter. Stir in egg. Add potato; mix well. Stir in lemon rind and juice; mix thoroughly.

Mrs. Paul F. (Rose) Newpower
St. Paul, Minnesota

Pecan Pie Cookies

Miniature pecan pies that will delight hostess and guest alike. They're beautiful little pastries that are much easier than they look, and taste as good as they look!

1 cup butter or margarine
½ cup sugar
½ cup dark corn syrup
2 eggs, separated
2½ cups flour, unsifted

Pecan Filling:
½ cup powdered sugar
¼ cup butter or margarine
3 tablespoons dark corn syrup
½ cup chopped pecans

Cream butter, gradually add sugar on low speed of mixer. Add corn syrup and egg yolks; beat until blended.

Stir in flour. Chill several hours.

Using 1 tablespoon of dough for each cookie, roll into balls. Brush very lightly with slightly beaten egg whites. Place on greased cookie sheet.

Bake at 375° for 5 minutes. Remove from oven.

Roll ½ teaspoon of chilled Pecan Filling into a ball and press firmly into the center of each cookie. Return to oven; bake 5 minutes longer or until lightly browned. Cool 5 minutes on cookie sheet; remove then cool completely on rack. Makes about 4 dozen.

Pecan Filling

Combine sugar, butter and corn syrup in saucepan; stir to blend.

Cook over medium heat, stirring occasionally, until mixture reaches a full boil. Remove from heat; stir in pecans. Chill.

Joanne Wacek
Albuquerque, New Mexico

Prize Teacake Surprises

A chocolate candy kiss is molded into the center of these delicious cookies. They're easier than they look, in fact, they can even be done successfully in a microwave oven.

1 cup butter
1 egg
1 teaspoon vanilla
½ cup confectioners' sugar
2½ cups flour
1 cup finely chopped pecans
1 9-oz. pkg. milk chocolate kisses
Confectioners' sugar

In mixing bowl, soften butter for 10 - 15 seconds in microwave or have at room temperature. Add egg, vanilla and ½ cup confectioners' sugar; beat until light and fluffy.

Blend in flour and nuts. Shape dough (about the size of walnut) around each chocolate kiss.

Bake at 325° for 15 to 20 minutes. To microwave, place 12 balls at a time on 2 thicknesses of paper towels. Cook about 1 minute, 45 seconds — or until surface no longer looks doughy.

Carefully remove to shallow bowl of confectioners' sugar. Roll while hot; cool, then roll again. Makes about 4 dozen.

Marilyn Martell
Debbie Martell
Thousand Oaks, California

Marilyn Martell, *County Fair Prize Cookies*, Prize Publishers, P. O. Box 281, Port Hueneme, California. Used by permission of Prize Publishers.

Carmel Nut Acorns

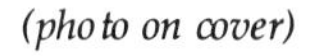

Very clever acorn-shaped cookies that are sure to be conversation pieces. And, besides being cute and clever, they're just plain good!

1 cup butter
3/4 cup brown sugar
2 teaspoons vanilla
2 1/2 cups flour
1 teaspoon baking powder
1/2 cup chopped pecans
Carmel Nut Topping:
1/2 lb. carmel candies
1/4 cup water
3/4 cup chopped pecans

Cream butter and brown sugar. Add vanilla and dry ingredients; mix well. Stir in 1/2 cup pecans.

Shape into oval balls, about 1-inch in diameter, to resemble acorns. Place on ungreased cookie sheet.

Bake at 325° for 15-18 minutes. Remove to wire rack and cool thoroughly.

Melt carmels with water in the top of a double boiler, stirring to make a smooth mixture.

Dip the large end of the acorn cookies in the carmel sauce and then in the chopped nuts. Return to wire racks to dry.

Makes about 3 1/2 to 4 dozen cookies.

Mrs. Clifford Sayre
Minneapolis, Minnesota

Snappy Turtle Cookies

These clever turtle-shaped cookies really make a hit with the small-fry!

½ cup margarine
½ cup brown sugar
1 egg
1 egg yolk
¼ teaspoon vanilla
⅛ teaspoon maple flavoring
1½ cups flour
¼ teaspoon soda
¼ teaspoon salt
Pecan halves

Cream margarine, add sugar and cream well. Add egg and yolk, beat well. Blend in flavorings.

Add dry ingredients, mix.

Arrange pecan halves in groups of three on greased baking sheet. Mold dough into balls. Dip bottoms into egg white and press onto nuts.

Bake at 350° for 10 minutes. Cool and frost.

Creamy Chocolate Frosting

1/3 cup chocolate chips
¼ cup milk
1 tablespoon margarine
1 cup powdered sugar

Combine chocolate, milk and margarine. Heat slowly til chocolate melts. Blend well.

Remove from heat, add sugar and beat well.

Vicki Green
Albuquerque, New Mexico

Chocolate Nut Lollypops

Cute and clever – these cookies always make a hit with children.

½ cup butter or margarine
½ cup shortening
1 cup sugar
1 egg
1 teaspoon vanilla
2 squares unsweetened chocolate, melted and cooled
2 cups sifted flour
¼ cup cornstarch
1 teaspoon baking powder
½ teaspoon salt
1 cup chopped walnuts
1 6-oz. pkg. semi-sweet chocolate chips, melted
1 cup finely chopped, lightly toasted almonds

Cream butter, shortening and sugar. Add egg and vanilla; beat until fluffy. Add cooled chocolate.

Sift together dry ingredients. Add to creamed mixture in 2 parts and mix well. Stir in chopped nuts. Chill dough 1 hour.

Shape in balls the size of large walnuts. Place 4 inches apart on greased cookie sheet, staggering rows. Press with flat-bottomed glass covered with plastic wrap. Insert short narrow meat sticks over half-way through center of cookies.

Bake at 350° for 10 to 12 minutes or until done. Carefully remove to racks to cool.

Spread with melted chips and sprinkle with chopped almonds. Let cool on wax paper.

Marilyn Martell
Thousand Oaks, California

Marilyn Martell, *County Fair Prize Cookies*, Prize Publishers, P. O. Box 281, Port Hueneme, California. Used by permission of Prize Publishers.

All-American Lollypop Cookies

These cookies look like miniature old-fashioned all-day suckers that will delight children of all ages.

1 cup shortening
3 oz. cream cheese, softened
1 cup sugar
1 egg white
1 teaspoon vanilla
½ teaspoon peppermint extract
2½ cups flour
½ teaspoon salt
¼ teaspoon baking powder
Red and blue food coloring

Cream shortening and cream cheese; add sugar and beat until fluffy. Add egg white and flavorings; mix well.

Stir in sifted dry ingredients until well blended. Divide dough in 3 portions. Add red food color to 1st part, blue to 2nd, and leave 3rd plain. Wrap separately and chill ½ hour or until easy to handle.

Work with small portions of dough at a time. Roll with hands ½ teaspoon of each color of dough into narrow rope-like shapes. Place 3 colors side-by-side on lightly greased cookie sheet. Press together and roll lightly with hands to make 1 single rope shape. Coil, twisting gently, into a circle shape of size desired. Leave about 3″ between cookies, staggering rows. Insert narrow meat sticks through ¾ of cookie.

Bake at 350° for 8 to 12 minutes or until set but not browned. Cool slightly; remove carefully to paper towel covered racks. When cool, wrap in plastic wrap and tie with colored narrow ribbons.

Note: If desired, before baking brush cookies with slightly beaten egg white and sprinkle with granulated sugar.

Marilyn Martell
Thousand Oaks, California

Marilyn Martell, *County Fair Prize Cookies*, Prize Publishers, P. O. Box 281, Port Hueneme, California. Used by permission of Prize Publishers.

Candy Cane Cookies

These clever red and white Candy Cane Cookies will delight young and old alike at Christmastime.

1 cup shortening (may be part butter or margarine)
2 cups sifted confectioners' sugar
1 egg
1½ teaspoons vanilla
1½ teaspoons almond extract
2½ cups flour
½ teaspoon salt
1 teaspoon red food coloring
½ cup crushed peppermint candy
½ cup sugar

Cream shortening, confectioners' sugar, egg, vanilla and almond extract until light.

Sift flour and salt together; stir into creamed mixture.

Divide dough in half. Color one half the dough with red food coloring, leaving the other half white. Add peppermint candy to white portion of dough.

Roll 1 teaspoon of dough into strips about 5 inches long. Place 1 red strip alongside 1 white strip; press together lightly and twist like a rope. Place on cookie sheet. Sprinkle candy canes with ½ cup granulated sugar.

Bake at 375° for 8 to 10 minutes or until firm.

Mrs. Virginia Huber
Tujunga, California

Heavenly Holiday Cookies

"The texture of these super cookies is like a 'Pecan Sandie'," states Trudy Richardson. "And, they're so nice to keep in the refrigerator over the holidays for unexpected guests. It takes only a few minutes and you're serving fresh, hot Christmas cookies!"

1 cup shortening
1 cup butter or margarine
2 cups sugar
1 teaspoon soda
1 tablespoon corn syrup
3 eggs
5 cups flour
1 cup chopped pecans
1 cup red and green candied cherries, chopped
1 cup chopped dates or raisins

Cream shortening, butter and sugar until light. Add remaining ingredients, one at a time, in order given. Mix in fruits and nuts by hand.

Form into 5 or 6 rolls; wrap in waxed paper. Chill 1 hour or up to 3 weeks in the refrigerator (or in the freezer for a longer period of time).

Slice ¼-inch thick and place 1½-inches apart on ungreased cookie sheets.

Bake at 375° for 12 minutes.

Mrs. Kirk (Trudy) Richardson
Omaha, Nebraska

Blue Ribbon Cream Puffs

This is really a prize-winning recipe! These delectable puffs have won Blue Ribbons for Marilyn Martell, her children, and her husband!

1 cup water
½ cup butter
¼ teaspoon salt
1 cup flour, sifted
4 large eggs

In medium saucepan, slowly bring water with butter and salt to boiling. Remove from heat.

With wooden spoon, beat in flour all at once.

Return to low heat; continue beating until mixture forms a ball and leaves side of pan. Remove from heat.

Beat in eggs, one at a time, beating vigorously after each addition until mixture is smooth. Continue beating until dough is shiny and satiny and breaks in strands, about 8 - 10 minutes.

Drop by rounded tablespoonfuls, 2-inches apart, onto ungreased cookie sheet.

Bake at 400° for 30 minutes, then reduce temperature to 375° and continue baking for 20 minutes or until puffed and golden. Puffs should sound hollow when lightly tapped with fingertip. Cool completely on wire rack, away from drafts.

With sharp knife, cut off tops crosswise. Carefully remove any pieces of soft dough. Fill; replace top and dust with confectioners' sugar or glaze with a thin chocolate frosting.

French Cream Filling

1 3-oz. pkg. cream cheese
1/3 cup confectioners' sugar, sifted
½ teaspoon vanilla
2 cups heavy cream, whipped

Cream cream cheese; slowly add confectioners' sugar and vanilla. Fold in whipped cream.

Marilyn Martell
Thousand Oaks, California

Marilyn Martell, *Prize-Winning Desserts*, Prize Publications, P. O. Box 281, Port Hueneme, California. Used by permission of Prize Publications.

Luscious Lemon Cream Puffs

"Cream Puffs are an elegant dessert that my family raves about, and, they're superb for special occasions, too!," states Genevieve Palmer. "And," she advises, "they're so easy! There's no need to be afraid to try something you always thought was impossible!"

½ cup butter
1 cup boiling water
1 cup all-purpose flour
¼ teaspoon salt
4 large eggs

Melt the butter in boiling water. Add the flour and salt all at once. Stir vigorously.

Cook over low heat, stirring constantly until the mixture forms a ball that doesn't separate. (This takes 1 or 2 minutes). Remove from heat and cool slightly.

Add eggs, one at a time, beating hard after each addition until mixture is smooth.

Drop dough by tablespoons 2½ to 3-inches apart onto lightly greased cookie sheet.

Bake at 450° for 15 minutes. Reduce heat and bake at 325° for 25 minutes. Remove from cookie sheet and cool on rack away from drafts.

Cut off tops and remove any filament. Fill with lemon filling, sweetened whipped cream or as desired. Chill. Dust with confectioners' sugar just before serving.

Lemon Filling

¾ cup sugar
3 tablespoons cornstarch
¼ teaspoon salt
3 egg yolks, slightly beaten
¾ cup water
1 tablespoon butter
1/3 cup lemon juice
1 teaspoon grated lemon rind
1 cup heavy cream, whipped
1½ tablespoons sugar
½ teaspoon vanilla

Blend sugar, cornstarch and salt in saucepan. Combine egg yolks and water; stir into sugar mixture. Cook over medium heat, stirring constantly, until mixture comes to a boil. Boil 1 minute. Remove from heat.

Add butter, lemon juice and lemon rind; stir until blended. Cool. Fold in sweetened whipped cream. Fill cream puffs.

Genevieve Palmer
Salt Lake City, Utah

Cookies with a foreign flavor

Viennese Walnut Cookies

(photo on cover)

A superb European pastry! A very delicious, and very pretty cookie from a great cook who takes pride and great care in everything she bakes.

½ cup butter
1/3 cup granulated sugar
¼ teaspoon salt
1 teaspoon vanilla
1 egg yolk
1¼ cups sifted flour
1-1/3 cups finely chopped walnuts
Buttercream Frosting
Walnut Halves

Cream butter, sugar, salt and vanilla together until light and creamy. Add egg yolk and beat well.

Blend in flour and walnuts.

Using hands, form dough into a ball. Chill 30 minutes. Roll on lightly floured board to a little less than ¼-inch thick. Cut with 2-inch cookie cutter.

Bake at 350° on ungreased cookie sheets for 10 to 12 minutes or until very lightly browned. Cool on wire racks.

Put 2 cookies together with Buttercream Frosting tinted pink or green. Top with a swirl of frosting and decorate with a walnut half.

Buttercream Frosting

2 cups sifted powdered sugar
2 tablespoons butter, melted
½ teaspoon vanilla
Milk

Blend powdered sugar, butter and vanilla with enough milk to make of spreading consistency. Tint pink or green, if desired.

Mrs. Wallace Anderson
Colon, Nebraska

Kifli

(photo on cover)

A delectable "Old-World" pastry rich in sour cream, walnuts and almond flavoring – a very special cookie for those very special occasions. Expensive to make, but well worth it!

4 cups flour, unsifted
2 cups margarine
4 egg yolks, slightly beaten
1 cup dairy sour cream

Place flour in large bowl. With pastry blender, cut in margarine until mixture resembles coarse crumbs. Add egg yolks and sour cream; stir until combined.

Turn out on lightly floured surface and knead until dough is smooth and can be shaped into a ball. If too sticky, knead in more flour. (Dough can be refrigerated until ready to use).

On lightly floured surface, roll out one quarter of dough at a time, to measure 16 x 12-inches, 1/8-inch thick. With pastry wheel, cut into 2-inch squares.

Place a generous 1/2 teaspoon filling in the center of each square; then bring 2 opposite corners, overlapping, over filling; pinch corners together to seal. Place on cookie sheets. Brush lightly with egg.

Bake at 400° for 12 minutes, or until golden. Remove, and roll in confectioners' sugar. Let cool on wire rack. Makes 16 dozen.

Walnut Filling

1 1/4 lb. walnuts, ground
1 cup granulated sugar
1/2 cup milk
1 tablespoon almond extract

Combine ingredients; blend well.

Glaze

1 egg, beaten
Confectioners' sugar

Joni Jensen
Provo, Utah

Rosettes

(photo on page 18)

These "Old-World" cookies look complicated, but they're so simple to make and simply delicious!

2 eggs
2 teaspoons sugar
1 cup milk
¼ teaspoon salt
1 cup flour
Hot oil for frying
Confectioners' sugar

Beat eggs slightly, blend in sugar until just barely mixed. Add milk; blend.

Sift salt and flour together; stir into creamed mixture. Beat until as smooth as heavy cream.

Follow cooking directions with rosette iron set. Dust with confectioners' sugar. Makes about 3 dozen.

Mrs. Cyril Bauer
Harrisonville, Missouri

Krumkake

(photo on page 26)

The Swedish are unbeatable when it comes to making cookies and this is one of their best!

3 eggs
½ cup sugar
½ cup cold water
½ cup butter, melted and cooled
½ teaspoon vanilla
1 cup flour

Beat eggs with sugar until light. Add cold water, cooled butter, vanilla and flour. Stir until smooth.

Heat Krumkake iron over low heat; brush lightly with melted butter. Pour about 1 tablespoon of batter into iron. Cook wafer slowly until golden on one side; turn and cook on the other side. Remove each wafer with a fork and roll over cylinder. Dust with powdered sugar or fill with sweetened whipped cream and fruit mixture.

Mrs. Cyril Bauer
Harrisonville, Missouri

Pfeffernuesse

A German favorite that Americans love. They take a little more effort than most cookies, but they're worth the effort!

2 tablespoons butter
1¼ cups sifted powdered sugar
3 egg yolks
1 teaspoon grated lemon rind
¼ lb. candied citron
2 teaspoons crushed cardamon seed
¼ cup blanched almonds, finely chopped
2 cups flour
½ teaspoon baking soda
½ teaspoon salt
2 teaspoons cinnamon
½ teaspoon ground cloves
½ teaspoon nutmeg
⅛ teaspoon black pepper
3 egg whites

Glaze:
1½ cups sifted powdered sugar
3 tablespoons milk

Cream butter. Add sifted powdered sugar, then well-beaten egg yolks and lemon rind.

Chop citron fine. Stir citron, crushed cardamon and almonds into dry ingredients which have been sifted together three times.

Add flour mixture to creamed ingredients. Beat egg whites until stiff and fold into batter. Chill one hour.

Form small balls and place on waxed paper. Let stand overnight. Brush cookies all over top and sides with glaze. Place balls on greased cookie sheet.

Bake at 375° for 15 minutes. Makes 4 dozen.

Marilyn Martell
Thousand Oaks, California

Marilyn Martell, *County Fair Prize Cookies*, Prize Publications, P. O. Box 281, Port Hueneme, California. Used by permission of Prize Publications.

Rosettes p. 17

Danish Cookies

The Danish love to top their cookies with a creamy mixture of sweetened whipped cream and cream cheese then they add a dab of raspberry jam. Delectable!

1 cup sugar
1 cup shortening
1 egg
2 cups flour
½ teaspoon baking soda
¼ teaspoon cream of tartar
1 teaspoon vanilla or almond extract

Cream sugar, shortening and egg until light.

Sift dry ingredients together; stir into creamed mixture. Add flavoring; mix well.

Form into small balls.

Bake at 400° until slightly browned.

Mrs. Virginia Huber
Tujunga, California

Swedish Almond Cookies

Traditionally served during the holidays in Sweden, these cookies make a beautiful addition to any elegant cookie tray.

1 cup butter
½ cup sifted powdered sugar
2¼ cups flour
1 teaspoon salt
1 teaspoon almond extract
½ cup blanched almonds, ground
2 tablespoons granulated sugar
1 egg white, slightly beaten

Cream butter and powdered sugar.

Stir in flour, salt, almond extract and mix well. Chill.

Shape dough into fingers. Mix together almonds and granulated sugar. Roll fingers in egg white, then in nut mixture.

Bake at 350° for 12-14 minutes.

Kathy Koenig
Orange County, California

Chinese Almond Fair Cookies

So authentic – they're made with rice flour – and so good! Gung hay fat choy!

¾ cup butter (don't substitute)
¾ cup shortening
1 cup sugar
1 egg
1 teaspoon almond extract
1½ cups rice flour
1½ cups flour
½ teaspoon salt
1 egg yolk
1 teaspoon water
Almonds, blanched and lightly browned

Cream butter and shortening; add sugar and beat until fluffy. Add egg and almond extract; mix well.

Add sifted dry ingredients. Mix until blended.

Shape into 1" balls; flatten a little. Brush with egg yolk and water. Press almond in center.

Bake at 350° for 15 to 20 minutes. Remove to wire racks. Cool.

Marilyn Martell
Thousand Oaks, California

———————

Marilyn Martell, *County Fair Prize Cookies,* Prize Publications, P. O. Box 281, Port Hueneme, California. Used by permission of Prize Publishers.

Italian Almond Stix

This Italian cookie has become a tradition and a "must" for the holiday season in the Pietromonaco family. They can be made ahead of the busy holiday season as they will stay crisp for a long time if stored in an air-tight container. And, "they're just great for dunking!," states Fran Pietromonaco.

4 cups all-purpose flour
1 tablespoon baking powder
1¼ cups powdered sugar
1 teaspoon salt
¾ cup unsalted butter
4 large eggs, beaten
2 teaspoons pure anise flavoring
2 cups slivered almonds, toasted

Sift dry ingredients together; set aside.

Cream butter in large bowl. Make a well in the center; add the eggs and anise flavoring, blending in well with a wooden spoon.

Add flour, gradually blending in from the center out. Stir in almonds.

Divide dough into 4 parts. Pat dough into oblong shapes. Place dough on 2 greased and floured cookie sheets with sides, 2½ to 3 inches apart.

Bake at 375° for 12 minutes. Remove from oven. Using a sharp knife, cut cookies ½-inch wide at an angle. Turn each cookie over and return to oven and bake until golden or light brown.

Fran Pietromonaco
Orange, California

Drommar
(Dream Cookies)

The secret to these very light European butter cookies is the use of ammonium carbonate instead of baking powder. Ammonium carbonate can be purchased at your local drugstore.

1 cup sugar
1 cup butter
2 teaspoons vanilla sugar
2½ cups sifted flour
½ teaspoon ammonium carbonate

Cream butter and sugar until light and fluffy.

Combine the vanilla sugar, flour and ammonium carbonate; blend into butter mixture.

Shape dough into small balls; place on cookie sheet.

Bake at 300° for 20 to 25 minutes. Cookies should have a very pale color and rounded cracked tops.

Mrs. Ralph A. Ochs
Vallejo, California

Marshmallow Ribbon Brownies p. 27

Biscochitos

A Spanish Cookie in the French Fleur de Lis shape that is traditionally served at Christmas or at fancy teas. The secret to success for these delicate cookies is real lard, so don't be tempted to make a substitution.

1 lb. pure lard
1½ cups sugar
2 eggs
2 teaspoons anise
6½ cups flour
3 teaspoons baking powder
1 teaspoon salt
½ cup orange juice, wine or brandy
½ cup sugar
1 teaspoon cinnamon

Cream lard; add sugar gradually, creaming well. Add eggs and anise, cream thoroughly.

Sift dry ingredients together; stir into creamed mixture. Add orange juice, wine or brandy; blend well.

Knead slightly and roll out to ¼-inch thickness on floured board. Cut into Fleur de Lis design and other fancy shapes. Mix ½ cup sugar and cinnamon; dust top of each cookie with cinnamon-sugar mixture.

Bake at 350° for 10 minutes.

Frances L. Holmes
Albuquerque, New Mexico

French Butter Creams

These very light, delicate cookies received the first prize at the California State Fair two years in a row. They're a traditional Christmas cookie so good that you'll have requests to bake them for other special occasions, too!

½ cup butter
½ cup shortening
1½ cups powdered sugar, sifted
¼ teaspoon salt
1 teaspoon vanilla
1 egg
2 cups flour, sifted
1 teaspoon soda
1 teaspoon cream of tartar

Cream butter and shortening. Add powdered sugar gradually; beat until light. Add salt, vanilla and egg; beat thoroughly.

Sift flour, soda and cream of tartar together; add to creamed mixture. Chill at least 10 minutes and preferably 1 hour.

Form into ½-inch balls. Place on cookie sheet and flatten with fork dipped in sugar.

Bake at 350° for 13 minutes. Cool before removing from cookie sheet.

Lila Korvink
Sacramento, California

Mexican Sugar Cookies

The Mexican's love all their food spicy – even their cookies. These cinnamon spiced Mexican Sugar Cookies were awarded the Blue Ribbon 5 years in a row!

1 cup butter
½ cup powdered sugar
1 teaspoon vanilla
2¼ cups flour
1 teaspoon cinnamon
¼ cup granulated sugar
1/3 teaspoon cinnamon

Cream butter and powdered sugar. Blend in vanilla.

Sift flour and 1 teaspoon cinnamon together; stir into creamed mixture. Roll into 1-inch balls. Flatten between palms to ¼-inch.

Bake at 400° for 8 to 10 minutes. Mix granulated sugar and 1/3 teaspoon cinnamon. Roll cookies in sugar-cinnamon mixture while still hot.

Mary V. Woitt
Merced, California

Blue ribbon brownies

Marshmallow Ribbon Brownies

(photo on page 23)

These delectable brownies are the favorite of Alexander Schreiner, the organist for the famed Mormon Tabernacle Choir.

1 cup butter
1/3 cup cocoa
2 cups sugar
4 eggs
1½ cups flour
2 teaspoons vanilla
1½ cups chopped nuts
1 10-oz. pkg. minature marshmallows

Blend butter, cocoa and sugar. Beat in eggs, one at a time.

Stir in flour, vanilla and nuts. Pour into a greased 9 x 13-inch pan.

Bake at 350° for 20 to 25 minutes. Remove from oven and put marshmallows on top. Return to oven for 7 more minutes. Cool; frost with Cocoa Buttercream Frosting. Let stand 12 hours before cutting.

Cocoa Buttercream Frosting

¼ cup butter, softened
2½ to 3 cups powdered sugar
1/3 cup cocoa
1/3 cup cream
1 teaspoon vanilla

Cream butter, gradually add powdered sugar and cocoa with enough cream to make of spreading consistency. Stir in vanilla.

Margie Jensen
Provo, Utah

Krumkake p. 17

Chocolate Mint Brownies

Ramona Kenny frosts her brownies with candy! While the brownies are still warm from the oven she places candy mints on top, returns them to the oven for a few minutes, then spreads the candy frosting into swirls. Yummy!

2/3 cup shortening, melted
1 cup cocoa
½ cup evaporated milk
4 tablespoons water
2 cups sugar
2 tablespoons corn syrup
2 teaspoons vanilla
4 eggs
1½ cups flour
1 teaspoon baking powder
½ teaspoon salt
1 cup chopped nuts
Mints

Mix melted shortening and cocoa together. Stir in milk and water. Add sugar, corn syrup and vanilla, mixing well. Add eggs, one at a time, beating well after each addition.

Sift dry ingredients together; add to creamed mixture, beating until smooth. Stir in nuts.

Pour into greased 9 x 13-inch cooking sheet. (Batter is quite thin).

Bake at 350° for 30 minutes. Place chocolate fudge, butter cream or chocolate mints on top. Return to oven for a few minutes to melt mints. Spread or swirl frosting. Cool. Cut into squares. May also be served plain.

Ramona Kenny
Holden, Utah

Butterscotch Brownies

(photo on page 61)

Chewy butterscotch brownies on a brown sugar-rich coconut and pecan crust topped with a butterscotch glaze – nothing ordinary about these brownies!

¼ cup butter
1 cup flaked or shredded coconut
½ cup brown sugar, firmly packed
½ cup chopped pecans
1¾ cups flour, sifted
½ teaspoon soda
¼ teaspoon salt
¼ cup butter
1 cup brown sugar, firmly packed
1 egg, unbeaten
½ teaspoon vanilla
½ cup pecans
½ cup miniature marshmallows
1 cup miniature marshmallows

Melt the ¼ cup butter in saucepan. Stir in coconut, ½ cup brown sugar and ½ cup pecans. Spread in bottom of greased 13x9x2-inch pan; set aside.

Sift dry ingredients together; set aside.

Cream ½ cup butter, 1 cup brown sugar, egg and vanilla until light. Blend in dry ingredients. Stir in ½ cup pecans and marshmallows.

Spoon dough in small amounts over coconut mixture. Pat out evenly with floured hands.

Bake at 350° for 25 to 30 minutes, or until golden brown. If desired, sprinkle with 1 cup miniature marshmallows and bake an additional 1 to 2 minutes. Cool. Drizzle with glaze and cut into bars.

Butterscotch Glaze

1 tablespoon butter, melted
½ cup powdered sugar
¼ cup brown sugar
2 to 3 teaspoons milk, heated

Mix all ingredients together adding more milk if necessary to make the consistency of a glaze.

Joni Jensen
Provo, Utah

Blonde Brownies

A brownie without chocolate and with a meringue-nut topping. Very unusual and very good!

½ cup butter
1 cup sugar
1 egg yolk
1 whole egg
1 teaspoon vanilla
½ teaspoon salt
1 teaspoon baking powder
2 cups flour, sifted
Topping:
1 cup brown sugar
1 cup chopped walnuts
1 egg white, unbeaten

Cream butter and sugar until light. Add egg yolk, whole egg and vanilla; blend well.

Sift flour, baking powder, and salt together; add to creamed mixture, mixing well.

Pour into 9 x 9-inch greased pan. Combine topping ingredients and spread over batter.

Bake at 325° for 1 hour. Cut into squares.

Genevieve Palmer
Salt Lake City, Utah

Double Deck Brownies

One of the best brownie recipes made better by topping it with almond-flavored coconut. Delicious combination!

2/3 cup flour, sifted
½ teaspoon baking powder
¼ teaspoon salt
1 cup sugar
2 eggs, well-beaten
1/3 cup shortening, melted
1/3 cup coconut
½ teaspoon almond extract
1½ squares unsweetened chocolate, melted

Sift dry ingredients together; set aside.

Add sugar gradually to beaten eggs, beating thoroughly. Add shortening and blend well. Stir in flour mixture.

Turn ¼ of batter into a small bowl. Add coconut and almond extract; mix well. Add chocolate to remaining batter.

Spread chocolate batter evenly in a greased 8 x 8 x 2-inch pan. Drop coconut batter by teaspoonful over chocolate batter in pan; spread carefully to form a thin even layer.

Bake at 350° for 35 minutes, or until done.

Charlotte DeRosa
Oakland, California

Fudge-Nut Brownies

Shirley House found a recipe for Brownies in a newspaper column by a renowned chef. She changed it slightly and came up with a Brownie that won the Blue Ribbon 5 years in a row! This recipe has **never** *failed to take a ribbon!*

4 oz. unsweetened chocolate
1 cup butter, soft
2 cups sugar
3 eggs, slightly beaten
2 teaspoons vanilla
½ teaspoon salt
1 - 1¼ cups chopped nuts
1 cup flour, sifted

Melt chocolate in top of double boiler over hot water. Stir in butter.

Remove from heat, add sugar and blend. Add eggs; mix well. (Very sticky at this point). Add vanilla and salt. Stir in chopped nuts. Add flour and mix well. Pour into buttered and floured 9x9x2-inch pan.

Bake at 350° for 40 to 45 minutes.

Shirley A. House
Livermore, California

Blue Ribbon Date Brownies

Something new and special in brownies – moist date nuggets are added for extra interest.

½ cup butter
3 squares unsweetened chocolate
1-1/3 cups sugar
4 eggs, well beaten
1 teaspoon vanilla
1 cup flour
½ teaspoon baking powder
¼ teaspoon salt
1 cup coarsely chopped walnuts
1 cup cut-up dates
Creamy Chocolate Frosting
Pecan halves

In heavy saucepan, melt butter and chocolate over low heat; cool.

Add sugar gradually to eggs, beating thoroughly. Add chocolate mixture and vanilla; blend well.

Stir in sifted dry ingredients. Fold in walnuts and dates.

Bake at 350° in buttered foil-lined 9 x 13-inch pan for about 25 minutes. Cool slightly; lift out to rack. Spread with Creamy Chocolate Frosting. Decorate with pecan halves. Cool before cutting into 36 bars.

Creamy Chocolate Frosting

2 tablespoons butter
1 oz. unsweetened chocolate
1½ tablespoons warm water
1 cup confectioners' sugar, sifted

Melt butter and chocolate in heavy saucepan. Blend in warm water. Beat in confectioners' sugar until icing spreads easily.

Marilyn Martell
Thousand Oaks, California

Marilyn Martell, *Selected Cookie Gems*, Prize Publications, P. O. Box 281, Port Hueneme, California. Used by permission of Prize Publications.

Chewy Brownies

The secret to these moist brownies is the addition of a can of chocolate syrup!

½ cup butter
1 cup sugar
4 eggs
1 teaspoon vanilla
1 can chocolate syrup
1 cup plus 1 tablespoon flour
½ teaspoon baking powder
½ cup coarsely chopped nuts

Cream butter and sugar until light. Add eggs, two at a time, beating well after each addition. Blend in chocolate syrup.

Sift flour and baking powder together; stir into creamed mixture. Stir in nuts. Pour into jelly-roll pan or cookie sheet.

Bake at 350° for approximately 30 minutes. Frost when cool.

Fudge Frosting

6 tablespoons butter
6 tablespoons milk
1½ cups sugar
½ cup semi-sweet chocolate chips

Combine butter, milk and sugar in saucepan. Bring to boil; continue boiling for 30 seconds. Remove from heat and stir in chocolate chips.

Kay M. Ness
Minot, North Dakota

Fudge Nut Bars

(photo on page 49)

A favorite in our test kitchen. These crunchy oatmeal bars have a creamy chocolate filling that made a hit with everyone!

1 cup butter or margarine
1 cup brown sugar
2 eggs, beaten
2 teaspoons vanilla
2½ cups sifted flour
1 teaspoon soda
1 teaspoon salt
3 cups quick-cooking oats

Creamy Chocolate Filling:
1 - 12-oz. pkg. milk chocolate chips
1 can sweetened condensed milk
2 tablespoons butter
½ teaspoon salt
2 teaspoons vanilla
1 cup chopped nuts

Cream butter and sugar. Mix in eggs and vanilla.

Sift flour, soda and salt together. Stir oats into flour. Add dry ingredients to creamed mixture. Press 2/3 of mixture in bottom of jelly roll pan. Let stand while you make filling.

Filling: Combine chocolate chips, sweetened condensed milk, butter and salt in top of double boiler. Place over boiling water and stir until smooth. Add vanilla and nuts.

Spread filling over flour mixture in pan. Top with remaining flour mixture.

Bake at 350° for 30 minutes. Cut into bars.

Ramona Kenney
Holden, Utah

English Toffee Bars

A favorite with the Martell family and friends lucky enough to be treated to a sample. This crunchy, buttery cookie was the first of many Blue Ribbon cookies for Marilyn Martell. Now she's won so many ribbons that she's compiled them into a cookbook, **County Fair Prize Cookies.**

1 cup soft butter
1 cup sugar
1 egg, separated
2 cups sifted flour
1 teaspoon cinnamon
1½ cups chopped pecans or walnuts

Cream butter and sugar until smooth. Add egg yolk and mix well.

Add flour sifted with cinnamon, using hands to blend lightly. Spread in an even layer over entire surface of buttered 10″ x 15″ x 1″ cookie sheet.

Beat egg white slightly, spread on top. Sprinkle nuts over all, pressing into dough.

Bake at 275° for 1 hour. Cut into 1″ x 2″ bars or diamond shapes while very warm. Cool on rack.

Marilyn Martell
Thousand Oaks, California

Marilyn Martell, *County Fair Prize Cookies,* Prize Publishers, P. O. Box 281, Port Hueneme, California. Used by permission of Prize Publishers.

Toffee-Nut Bars

Toffee Nut Bars were included in the plate of prize-winning cookies Mrs. Brockhoff presented to the Mayor on TV. These cookies are good enough to impress anyone!

½ cup shortening (half butter)
½ cup brown sugar
1 cup flour, sifted
2 eggs
1 cup brown sugar
1 teaspoon vanilla
2 tablespoons flour
1 teaspoon baking powder
½ teaspoon salt
1 cup moist shredded coconut
1 cup chopped nuts

Cream shortening and ½ cup brown sugar thoroughly. Stir in 1 cup flour. Press and flatten with hand to cover bottom of ungreased 13 x 9-inch pan. Bake 10 minutes at 350°. Then spread with topping.

To make topping, beat the eggs, stir in 1 cup brown sugar and vanilla. Mix well. Combine 2 tablespoons flour, baking powder and salt. Stir into egg mixture. Add coconut and nuts.

Spread over first mixture, return to oven and bake 25 minutes at 350°. Cool slightly and cut into bars.

Mrs. Stephen Brockhoff
Hiawatha, Kansas

Chocolate Peanut Squares

A sure hit with the "Cookie Monster" set!

Crust:
½ cup butter
¼ cup brown sugar, firmly packed
¼ cup granulated sugar
1 egg yolk
½ teaspoon vanilla
¼ teaspoon salt
1 cup flour, sifted

Topping:
½ cup chocolate chips
1 egg white
½ cup brown sugar, firmly packed
1/3 cup salted peanuts, chopped

Cream butter. Add sugars and cream until light. Add egg yolk, vanilla, salt and flour; blend thoroughly. Pat firmly into bottom of 7 x 11 x ½-inch greased pan.

Bake at 350° for 15 minutes. Remove from oven and sprinkle with chocolate chips.

Beat egg white to soft peaks, add brown sugar. Spread on top of crust. Sprinkle with peanuts.

Bake 20 minutes more. Makes about 25 squares.

Kathy O'Neil
New Berlin, Wisconsin

Blue Ribbon Rocky Road Bars

A spectacular three-layer cream cheese cookie that is sure to win praises from your family and friends!

½ cup butter
1½ oz. unsweetened chocolate
1 cup sugar
2 eggs
1 teaspoon vanilla
1 cup flour
1 teaspoon baking powder
1 cup nuts, chopped

Melt butter and chocolate in saucepan over low heat. Blend in sugar, eggs and vanilla.

Sift dry ingredients; blend into chocolate mixture. Stir in nuts. Spread in greased 9 x 13-inch pan.

Filling

6 oz. cream cheese, softened
¼ cup soft butter
½ cup sugar
1 egg
½ teaspoon vanilla
2 tablespoons flour
¼ cup chopped nuts
1 6-oz. pkg. semi-sweet chocolate chips
2 cups mini-marshmallows (added after baking)

Cream cream cheese, butter, sugar, egg and vanilla until very smooth, creamy and fluffy. Stir in nuts and spread over chocolate layer. Sprinkle with chocolate chips.

Bake at 350° for 20 to 25 minutes or until toothpick inserted in center comes out clean. Sprinkle with marshmallows and bake 2 additional minutes.

Swirl frosting with marshmallows immediately after removing from oven. Cool in pan on cake rack. Cut into 36 or 42 bars.

Frosting

¼ cup butter
1½ oz. unsweetened chocolate
2 oz. cream cheese
¼ cup milk
1 lb. confectioners' sugar
1 teaspoon vanilla

Melt butter and chocolate in saucepan over low heat. Stir in cream cheese and milk. Add confectioners' sugar and beat until smooth and creamy. Blend in vanilla.

Marilyn Martell
Thousand Oaks, California

Marilyn Martell, *County Fair Prize Cookies,* Prize Publications, P. O. Box 281, Port Hueneme, California. Used by permission of Prize Publications.

Chocolate Chip-Macaroon Bars

A cookie everyone will love – especially the teenagers!

Crumb Crust:
1 cup flour
1/4 teaspoon soda
1/3 cup butter, softened
Macaroon Topping:
2 egg whites
1 tablespoon sugar
2 cups finely grated coconut
1/2 cup brown sugar, firmly packed
1/4 teaspoon salt
1 teaspoon vanilla
2 egg yolks
3/4 cup sweetened condensed milk
1/2 cup semi-sweet chocolate chips

Combine all ingredients for crust and blend until all particles are fine. Press into greased 7 x 11-inch pan.

Bake at 325° for 12 to 15 minutes - do not brown.

Beat egg whites until soft mounds form. Add sugar; continue beating until stiff peaks form. Fold in remaining ingredients.

Spread evenly over crust.

Bake for 25 to 30 minutes. Cool, then cut into bars. Makes 36 bars.

Sharon Dean
Orange County, California

Double Chocolate Bars

Double chocolaty and double good! And, so easy a 14-year-old captured the Sweepstakes with this recipe.

¼ cup butter
¾ cup granulated sugar
1 teaspoon vanilla
¼ cup light corn syrup
2 eggs
2 1-oz. squares chocolate, melted and cooled
1 cup sifted all-purpose flour
½ teaspoon salt
½ teaspoon baking powder
½ cup semisweet chocolate pieces
½ cup chopped California walnuts

Cream butter, sugar, and vanilla until fluffy. Add syrup and continue creaming. Beat in eggs and chocolate.

Sift together dry ingredients; stir into batter. Fold in chocolate pieces and walnuts. Spread in greased 9 x 9 x 2-inch baking pan.

Bake in a moderate oven 350° about 25 minutes. Cut in bars when cool.

Susan Herman
Sedalia, Missouri

Lemon Snowbars

Cecilia Peiffer is a full-time dental assistant who enjoys baking whenever she finds time, which is usually on the weekends. Weekends are special for her family because she always tries to bake at least one new or favorite recipe. Lemon Snowbars is one of her family's favorite weekend treats.

1 cup flour
¼ cup powdered sugar, sifted
½ cup butter
2 eggs
¾ cup granulated sugar
3 tablespoons lemon juice
2 tablespoons flour
¼ teaspoon baking powder
Powdered sugar

Combine flour and ¼ cup powdered sugar in bowl. Cut in butter until mixture clings together.

Pat into ungreased 8 x 8 x 2-inch baking pan.

Bake at 350° for 10 to 12 minutes.

Beat eggs, add granulated sugar and lemon juice. Beat until slightly thick and smooth (about 8-10 minutes).

Combine 2 tablespoons flour and baking powder; add to egg mixture, blending just until flour is moistened. Pour over baked layer.

Bake at 350° for 20 to 25 minutes. Sprinkle with sifted powdered sugar; cut into bars. Makes 20.

Cecilia Peiffer
Merced, California

Lemon Cheese Bars

Mrs. Pietromonaco has won three Blue Ribbons with this recipe that was given to her by an old friend. It makes a large batch (36 to 40 cookies) so she freezes some for later use. "These cookies freeze beautifully!," states Mrs. Pietromonaco. "They will keep up to three months in the freezer, if wrapped uncut after they're frozen."

1/3 cup margarine
1 cup plus 2 tablespoons flour
¼ cup brown sugar
Pinch of salt
¾ cup finely chopped pecans
8 oz. cream cheese
1 large egg
4 tablespoons brown sugar
½ teaspoon pure lemon flavoring
1 tablespoon fresh lemon juice
1 teaspoon grated lemon rind

Combine first 5 ingredients in a bowl and work with fingers until crumbly. Divide in half; press one half into an 8 x 8 x 2-inch square pan.

Bake at 350° for 15 minutes. Remove from oven and place on rack; cool about 8 to 10 minutes.

Beat remaining ingredients until well blended and creamy. Spread over baked crust; top with remaining crumb mixture.

Return to oven and bake again for 25 to 30 minutes. Cool completely then refrigerate. Cut into bars.

Fran Pietromonaco
Orange, California

Lemon Squares

"The fair judge liked these tangy lemon cookies so much she kept coming back for more, and I think you will, too!," states Mrs. Honnold.

Crust:
1 cup flour, sifted
½ cup soft butter
¼ cup confectioners' sugar
Filling:
2 eggs
1 cup granulated sugar
5 tablespoons lemon juice
2 tablespoons flour
½ teaspoon baking powder
Confectioners' sugar

Combine 1 cup flour, butter and confectioners' sugar. Press into ungreased 9 x 9-inch pan.

Bake at 300° for 20 minutes. Cool. (Crust will be firm but not browned).

Beat eggs slightly, add granulated sugar, lemon juice, 2 tablespoons flour and baking powder; mix well. Spread over crust.

Bake at 325° for 25 minutes. Remove from oven and sprinkle with confectioners' sugar. Refrigerate about 1 hour (this makes it easier to cut). Cut into 16 2-inch squares. Store in refrigerator, if they last that long.

Mrs. Sandy Honnold
Sutter Creek, California

Luscious Lemon Bars

"This recipe is exceptional!," states Catherine Crooks. "These lemon bars are delicate and very lemony with a tender crust. They will bring raves when served at receptions, showers, or any other star function!"

Crust:
1 cup soft butter
Dash salt
½ cup confectioners' sugar
2 cups flour

Filling:
¼ cup flour
2 cups granulated sugar
4 eggs, beaten
6 tablespoons lemon juice
Confectioners' sugar

Combine all the crust ingredients and mix well. Press into a greased 9 x 13-inch pan.

Bake at 350° for 15 minutes.

Combine 1/4 cup flour and granulated sugar; mix in beaten eggs and lemon juice. Pour onto slightly cooked crust.

Bake at 350° for 25 minutes or until set (edges will be browned before center is set). Cool; sprinkle with confectioners' sugar and cut into bars. Makes 3 dozen.

Catherine Crooks
Orem, Utah

Dream Bars

The Johannsen's (and just about everyone else) favorite cookie!

Crust:
1/4 cup shortening
1/4 cup butter
1/2 cup brown sugar, packed
1 cup flour

Topping:

2 eggs, well beaten
1 cup brown sugar, packed
1 teaspoon vanilla
2 tablespoons flour
1 teaspoon baking powder
1/2 teaspoon salt
1 cup moist shredded coconut
1 cup slivered almonds (or other nuts)

Combine sugars and shortening thoroughly. Stir in flour. Flatten into bottom of ungreased oblong pan, 13 x 9 x 2-inches.

Bake 10 minutes at 350°.

While crust is baking, prepare topping. Blend eggs, sugar and vanilla. Combine flour, baking powder and salt; add to egg mixture. Beat well. Stir in coconut and nuts. Spread over baked crust.

Bake for 25 minutes more, or until light brown. Cool and cut into bars.

Makes approximately 2 1/2 dozen 3″ x 1″ bars.

Mrs. Herman Johannsen
Artesian, South Dakota

Brown Sugar Chews

These cookies are chewy and soft when warm and firm when cooled.

1 egg
1 cup brown sugar, firmly packed
1 teaspoon vanilla
½ cup flour, sifted
¼ teaspoon salt
¼ teaspoon baking soda
1 cup chopped walnuts

Combine egg, brown sugar and vanilla; beat well.

Sift together the dry ingredients; stir into sugar mixture. Stir in nuts. Spread in greased 8-inch square pan.

Bake at 350° for 15 to 18 minutes. Cool in pan on rack, then cut into 1½-inch bars.

Grace Olmsted
Mitchell, South Dakota

Indian Bars

A Sweepstakes-winning recipe from the South Dakota State Fair!

1 cup butter or margarine
2 squares unsweetened chocolate
2 cups sugar
4 eggs, slightly beaten
1½ cups flour, sifted
1 teaspoon baking powder
2 teaspoons vanilla
1 cup chopped pecans

Melt butter and chocolate over low heat. Add sugar and eggs; mix thoroughly.

Sift flour with baking powder; stir into creamed mixture. Mix in vanilla and nuts. Pour into greased 9 x 13-inch pan.

Bake at 350° for 35 to 40 minutes. Cool completely on rack. Cut in 3 x 1½-inch bars. Makes about 2 dozen.

Grace Olmsted
Mitchell, South Dakota

Walnut Bars

These cookies keep so well that they even won the Blue Ribbon at the California State Fair when they were one week old!

1 cup whole wheat flour
2 cups brown sugar
¼ teaspoon salt
¼ teaspoon soda
2 eggs
1½ teaspoons vanilla
2 cups chopped walnuts

Combine all ingredients, except walnuts, in a mixing bowl. Mix until well blended. Fold in nuts.

Pour into greased 9 x 9-inch pan.

Bake at 350° for 20 to 25 minutes. Let stand until cool before cutting.

Suzanna Welton
Placerville, California

Deanna Sudweeks and Suzanna Welton, *Kitchen Magic,* p. 99. Used by permission.

Chocolate Mint Squares

Refreshing – and a delightful change from the usual Brownie recipe.

½ cup butter or margarine
½ cup brown sugar, firmly packed
1 egg, separated
1 6-oz. pkg. mint chocolate chips, chopped
1 teaspoon vanilla
¼ cup water
1 cup flour, sifted
Confectioners' sugar

Cream butter and sugar until light. Add egg yolk, chocolate pieces, vanilla, water, flour and mix well.

Beat egg white until stiff but not dry; fold into creamed mixture. Pour into greased 8 x 8 x 2-inch pan.

Bake at 375° for 25 to 30 minutes. Sprinkle top with powdered sugar.

Helen Solberg
Orange County, California

Choc-O-Chip Nut Squares

A delicious butter-rich cookie topped with a chocolate chip and nut meringue – very easy and very good!

½ cup butter
1 cup sugar
2 eggs, beaten
1½ cups flour
1 teaspoon baking powder
½ teaspoon salt

Topping:
½ cup nuts
½ pkg. chocolate chips
2 egg whites
1 cup brown sugar
½ teaspoon vanilla

Cream butter and sugar; blend in eggs.

Sift dry ingredients; stir into creamed mixture. Blend in vanilla.

Spread batter into buttered 9-inch pan. Sprinkle with nuts and chocolate chips.

Beat egg whites until stiff; slowly beat in brown sugar. Spread on top of batter, nuts and chocolate chips.

Bake at 325° for 30 minutes. Cool; cut into 1¼ x 1¼-inch squares.

Grace Olmsted
Mitchell, South Dakota

Caribbean Coconut Bars

Brown sugar rich coconut cookies that will be a favorite on any cookie tray.

4 eggs
1 lb. brown sugar
1½ teaspoons vanilla
1½ cups flour
2 teaspoons baking powder
½ teaspoon salt
1 cup chopped nuts
1 cup coconut

Blend eggs and brown sugar in top of double boiler; cook for 3 minutes. Remove from heat and add remaining ingredients.

Spread in lightly greased 9 x 13-inch pan.

Bake 20 minutes at 350°. Spread with thin powdered sugar icing or sprinkle with powdered sugar.

Doris Downs
Murray, Utah

Coconut Chews

The judges gave these delectable cookies a score of 100%. They'll also rate high when served at an afternoon tea or as a snack.

¼ cup shortening
¼ cup butter
½ cup brown sugar
1 cup flour, sifted
2 eggs, well beaten
1 cup brown sugar
1 teaspoon vanilla
2 tablespoons flour
1 teaspoon baking powder
½ teaspoon salt
1 cup moist shredded coconut
1 cup chopped walnuts or almonds

Bottom Layer

Cream shortening, butter and ½ cup brown sugar. Stir in 1 cup flour. Press and flatten with hand to cover the bottom of an ungreased 9 x 13-inch oblong pan.

Bake at 350° for 10 minutes then spread with topping.

Topping

Combine eggs, 1 cup brown sugar and vanilla; beat well. Combine baking powder, 2 tablespoons flour and salt; stir into egg mixture. Stir in coconut and nuts.

Return to oven and bake 25 minutes more at 350° or until topping is golden brown. Cool slightly then cut into bars. Makes about 2½ dozen 1″ x 3″ bars.

Kay Kernen
Arcata, California

Cherry-Coconut Bars

(photo on page 61)

So pretty – and so good! "Everyone loves them!," states Mrs. Strand, a very talented cook and Sweepstakes-winning flower arranger.

Pastry:
1 cup flour
½ cup margarine
3 tablespoons powdered sugar

Filling:
2 eggs
1 cup sugar
¼ cup flour
½ teaspoon baking powder
¼ teaspoon salt
1 teaspoon vanilla
½ cup chopped walnuts
½ cup flaked coconut
½ cup maraschino cherries, quartered
2 teaspoons maraschino cherry juice

Pastry: With hands, blend flour, margarine and powdered sugar until smooth (like a pie crust dough). Spread thin, using fingers, in lightly greased 7 x 11-inch pan.

Bake at 350° for 12 minutes.

Filling: Beat eggs until fluffy. Combine sugar, flour, baking powder and salt; add to beaten eggs, beating well. Add remaining ingredients; spread over baked pastry. (No need to cool pastry).

Bake at 350° for about 22 minutes. Cool; cut into bars.

Mrs. Phyllis A. Strand
St. Louis Park, Minnesota

Fudge Nut Bars p. 34

SCHOOL MORALE
Robert
4 Concepts in SCIENCE
Galaxies
Be home soon Love, mom

Meringue Topped Bar

Gloria Lenton LOVES to bake! She's always found an appreciative audience for her cookie baking as she comes from a family of 11 children! She now has 3 children of her own and the hired help on the farm who love her Meringue Topped Bars!

¾ cup soft butter
½ cup brown sugar
½ cup granulated sugar
3 egg yolks
1 teaspoon vanilla
2 cups flour
1 teaspoon baking powder
¼ teaspoon soda
¼ teaspoon salt
1 6-oz. pkg. chocolate chips
1 cup coconut
¾ cup nuts
3 egg whites
1 cup brown sugar

Cream butter and sugars until light. Blend in egg yolks and vanilla.

Sift dry ingredients together; stir into butter mixture. Batter will be stiff and crumbly.

Spread or press into a 12 x 18-inch cookie sheet. Sprinkle with chocolate chips, nuts and coconut.

Beat egg whites until fluffy and stiff. Beat in brown sugar. Spread over chocolate chips, nuts and coconut.

Bake at 325° to 350° for 35 to 45 minutes.

Gloria Lenton
Norwich, North Dakota

Apple Harvest Squares

This delicious dessert has that special flavor of European Bake Shoppe pastries that everyone loves!

1½ cups flour
1/3 cup sugar
¾ teaspoon salt
½ cup butter
4 cups sliced apples
2 tablespoons lemon juice
1/3 cup sugar
1 teaspoon cinnamon
½ cup sugar
1 egg
1/3 cup evaporated milk
1 teaspoon vanilla
¾ cup chopped nuts
1-1/3 cups flaked coconut

Mix together flour, 1/3 cup sugar and salt. Cut in butter until particles are fine. Press in bottom of 9 x 13-inch pan.

Sprinkle apples with lemon juice. Arrange over base. Combine 1/3 cup sugar and cinnamon; sprinkle over apples.

Bake at 375° for 20 minutes.

Combine ½ cup sugar, egg, evaporated milk, vanilla, nuts and coconut; spoon over apples.

Bake at 375° for 25 - 30 minutes. Cool. Cut into squares.

Melanie Sprecher
Wolsey, South Dakota

Apricot Squares

Unusually flavored and unusually good! Apricots, honey and nuts combine for a real taste-treat!

2 cups apricot nectar
2 cups dried apricots, cut in small pieces
½ cup chopped nuts
1/3 cup honey
1¼ cups flour, unsifted
½ teaspoon soda
¼ teaspoon salt
½ cup brown sugar, firmly packed
½ cup butter
1¼ cups old-fashioned rolled oats, uncooked

Mix together in saucepan the apricot nectar and the chopped apricots. Cook over medium heat, stirring occasionally, until thickened. Remove from heat and add nuts and honey. Cool.

In medium sized bowl, combine flour, soda, and salt. Stir in brown sugar. Cut in butter. Add oats; mix thoroughly.

Press one-half of oats mixture into a greased 8-inch square baking pan. Spoon apricot mixture over oat mixture. Top with remaining oat mixture, patting lightly.

Bake at 350° for 30 to 35 minutes. Cool. Cut into 16 squares.

Mrs. Randall Kirschman
La Canada, California

Waikiki Banana Bars

Shirley Crom's nine grandchildren can always look forward to their favorite banana cookies when they visit their grandmother.

¼ cup shortening
1 cup brown sugar, packed
½ teaspoon vanilla
½ teaspoon lemon extract
1 cup bananas, mashed
1½ cups sifted flour
1½ teaspoons baking powder
½ teaspoon salt
½ cup chopped walnuts
1/3 cup powdered sugar
1 teaspoon cinnamon

Combine the first 5 ingredients in the mixing bowl and beat thoroughly.

Sift dry ingredients together and add to creamed mixture, blending well. Stir in nuts.

Bake in greased 7 x 11-inch pan at 350° for 35 minutes, or until done. While warm, cut into bars and remove from pan. Combine powdered sugar and cinnamon; gently roll the warm bars in the mixture. Makes 20 to 24 bars.

Shirley Crom
Smartville, California

Pumpkin Nut Bars

If you like pumpkin pie, you'll love these pumpkin cookies!

½ cup shortening
2/3 cup pumpkin
1 cup flour
½ teaspoon baking powder
¼ teaspoon ginger
¼ teaspoon nutmeg
1 cup brown sugar
2 eggs
½ teaspoon soda
1 teaspoon cinnamon
½ cup chopped nuts
1 bar sweet chocolate
½ cup chopped nuts

Combine all ingredients except nuts and chocolate in large mixing bowl. Beat for 2 minutes at medium speed.

Stir in ½ cup nuts. Spread evenly in 9 x 13 x 2-inch pan.

Bake for 20 - 25 minutes at 350°. Frost with melted sweet chocolate; sprinkle with chopped nuts.

Helen Solberg
Orange County, California

Delicious Date Bars

The Lincoln's have a busy kitchen at fair time as Pat Lincoln and her two daughters all enjoy cooking and entering the competition. Three cooks in one kitchen can make things a little hectic, but it's worth it – the girls competed honorably in the 4-H division and Pat was awarded the Sweepstakes for her Delicious Date Bars!

¾ cup shortening (part margarine)
1 cup brown sugar, firmly packed
1¾ cups flour
½ teaspoon soda
1 teaspoon salt
1½ cups rolled oats

Cream shortening and sugar.

Blend flour, soda and salt together; stir into shortening mixture. Mix in rolled oats.

Flatten half of the mixture into the bottom of a greased 9 x 13-inch pan. Spread with cooled date filling. Top with remaining crumb mixture, patting lightly.

Bake at 400° for 25 to 30 minutes. While warm, cut into bars and remove from pan.

Makes about 2½ dozen 2 x 1½-inch bars.

Date Filling

3 cups cut-up dates
1½ cups water
¼ cup sugar

Combine ingredients in saucepan. Cook over low heat, stirring constantly until thickened, about 10 minutes. Cool.

Pat Lincoln
Grand Island, Nebraska

Delectable drop cookies

Hawaiian Moon Drops

(photo on page 56)

"Women seem to enjoy this cookie more than men," states Connie Saunders, "so I serve it at ladies luncheons and parties where it always makes a hit!"

2/3 cup shortening
¾ cup brown sugar
½ cup granulated sugar
2 eggs
3 cups flour
1 teaspoon baking powder
1 teaspoon soda
1 teaspoon salt
2/3 cup crushed pineapple, drained
1 teaspoon vanilla
¼ teaspoon lemon extract
1 cup chopped nuts

Cream shortening with sugars until light and fluffy. Add eggs, one at a time, beating well after each addition.

Sift dry ingredients together. Add to creamed mixture along with crushed pineapple, blending well. Add vanilla, lemon extract and nuts.

Drop by teaspoon onto greased cookie sheet.

Bake at 375° for 12 to 15 minutes. Frost with Pineapple Icing.

Pineapple Icing

½ cup pineapple juice
½ cup water
¼ cup cornstarch
2 tablespoons lemon juice
1 tablespoon butter
1 teaspoon vanilla
2 drops yellow food coloring
1½ cups powdered sugar, sifted
1½ cups shredded coconut

Combine pineapple juice, water and cornstarch in saucepan; cook over medium heat until thick. Add lemon juice, butter, vanilla and food coloring. Blend in powdered sugar.

Dip cookies into icing then into coconut.

Connie Saunders
Payson, Utah

Pecan Frosted Poppyseed Cookies

"I have nine children so I get lots of practice making cookies!," states Mrs. Seavers. However, her Archway Award-winning cookies "appeal more to older people than to children."

¾ cup butter
1-1/3 cups sugar
¼ cup light molasses
1 egg
1 cup pumpkin
1 teaspoon vanilla
2½ cups flour
1 teaspoon baking powder
1 teaspoon baking soda
¾ teaspoon salt
1/3 cup poppyseed
1 cup chopped pecans
Creamy Molasses Frosting
Pecan halves

Cream butter and sugar until light. Add molasses, egg, pumpkin and vanilla; blend well.

Sift dry ingredients together, stir into butter mixture. Add poppyseed and chopped pecans, stirring well.

Drop by rounded teaspoonful on greased cookie sheet.

Bake at 350° for 10 to 12 minutes. Frost with Creamy Molasses Frosting when cool. Decorate with pecan halves.

Creamy Molasses Frosting

¼ cup butter
2 cups powdered sugar
1 teaspoon cinnamon
1 tablespoon light molasses
1 tablespoon cream
¼ cup chopped pecans

Blend all ingredients, except pecans, until smooth and of spreading consistency. Stir in pecans.

Mrs. Jeanette Seavers
Stevens Point, Wisconsin

Creamy Orange Drops

Cream cheese makes these cookies a consistent Blue Ribbon winner.

1 cup softened butter
2 - 3 oz. packages softened cream cheese
1-1/3 cups sugar
1 - 6 oz. can unsweetened orange juice concentrate
2 teaspoons grated orange rind
2 eggs
2½ cups sifted flour
½ teaspoon baking soda
1 teaspoon baking powder
½ teaspoon salt
1 cup chopped pecans
Pecan halves

Combine butter, cream cheese and sugar until creamy. Stir in orange concentrate and rind. Add eggs; beat until fluffy.

Gradually sift in dry ingredients. Mix only until blended. Stir in chopped nuts. Drop by teaspoons onto well-buttered cookie sheet.

Bake at 350° for 10-12 minutes. Carefully remove warm cookies to wire rack. Glaze with orange frosting and decorate with pecan halves. Makes 5 dozen.

Marilyn Martell
Thousand Oaks, California

Applesauce Spice Cookies

Mrs. DeSpain's mother used to make these cookies for her when she was a child. Now she's making them for her children and all agree, "they're the best applesauce cookies!"

1 cup butter or margarine
1 cup granulated sugar
1 cup brown sugar, well packed
3 eggs
2 cups applesauce
2 teaspoons soda
4 cups flour, sifted
½ teaspoon salt
1 teaspoon nutmeg
1½ teaspoons cinnamon
½ teaspoon cloves
1 cup nuts or raisins

Cream butter and sugars. Add eggs and beat until fluffy.

Add soda to applesauce. Sift dry ingredients together. Add dry ingredients alternately with applesauce to butter mixture, blending well. Add raisins or nuts or a combination of both.

Drop by teaspoons onto greased baking sheets.

Bake at 400° for about 12 minutes or until done. Do not overbake.

Edie DeSpain
Granger, Utah

Frosted Applesauce-Nut Cookies

These saucy cookies won the first prize at the California State Fair!

½ cup shortening
½ cup brown sugar
½ cup granulated sugar
1 egg
2 cups flour, sifted
¼ teaspoon baking powder
¼ teaspoon soda
¼ teaspoon salt
¼ teaspoon cinnamon
½ cup applesauce
¼ cup raisins
½ cup chopped nuts
1 teaspoon vanilla

Cream shortening and sugar until light. Add egg; beat thoroughly.

Sift flour, baking powder, soda, salt and cinnamon together; stir into creamed mixture, blending well.

Add applesauce, raisins, nuts and vanilla; blend well. Drop by teaspoonfuls onto cookie sheet about 1½-inches apart.

Bake at 400° about 10 minutes or until light brown. Cool; frost with buttercream-powered sugar icing.

Lila L. Korvink
Sacramento, California

Starlight Mint Surprise Cookies

Mint-lovers will love this one!

3 cups flour
1 teaspoon soda
½ teaspoon salt
1 cup sugar
1 cup soft butter
½ cup brown sugar, firmly packed
2 eggs
1 teaspoon vanilla
2 6½ oz. pkgs. chocolate mint candy wafers
Walnut halves

Combine all ingredients except candy wafers and walnuts in a large bowl. Mix at lowest speed of mixer until dough forms.

Drop by teaspoonfuls onto ungreased cookie sheet. Press candy wafer on top of each. Cover with a scant teaspoonful of dough. Top each with a walnut half; smooth edges.

Bake at 375° for 9 - 12 minutes.

Mrs. Karen Isenhart
Decatur, Illinois

Blue Ribbon Molasses Cookies

An old-fashioned cookie with old-fashioned flavor. And, it's even more delicious when topped with the Creamy Frosting, chopped nuts and cherries that helped it win the Blue Ribbon at the Ventura County Fair.

1/3 cup soft butter
½ cup brown sugar
1 egg
½ cup molasses
2 cups flour
½ teaspoon soda
½ teaspoon baking powder
½ teaspoon salt
1 teaspoon cinnamon
½ teaspoon cloves
½ cup buttermilk
Creamy Frosting
Chopped nuts
Cherry halves

Cream butter and sugar until fluffy. Add egg and molasses; beat well.

Sift dry ingredients together. Add to sugar mixture alternately with buttermilk.

Drop by teaspoon onto greased cookie sheet.

Bake at 350° for 8 to 10 minutes.

Glaze while warm with Creamy Frosting. Decorate with chopped nuts and cherry halves. Makes about 4 dozen.

Creamy Frosting

2 tablespoons butter
¼ cup shortening
1 pkg. powdered sugar, sifted
¼ cup light cream
1 teaspoon vanilla
1 tablespoon white corn syrup

Cream butter and shortening until smooth. Add powdered sugar alternately with light cream.

Stir in vanilla and corn syrup. Beat until creamy.

Marilyn Martell
Thousand Oaks, California

Marilyn Martell, *County Fair Prize Cookies*, Prize Publishers, P. O. Box 281, Port Hueneme, California. Used by permission of Prize Publishers.

Butterscotch Brownies p. 29
Chocolate Drop Cookies p. 64
Cherry-Coconut Bars p. 48

Prize Pumpkin Spice Drops

These prize-winning cookies have received more than a fair share of awards. They received the Blue Ribbon at the Ventura County Fair, the California State Fair, and were featured in an article in the **Los Angeles Times.**

2 teaspoons soda
2 cups canned pumpkin
1 cup butter or margarine
2 cups brown sugar
4 eggs
3½ cups flour
1 teaspoon salt
1 teaspoon baking powder
2 teaspoons cinnamon
2 teaspoons nutmeg
1 teaspoon allspice
1 teaspoon pumpkin pie spice
Orange Filling
Nut Topping

Add soda to pumpkin; stir and set aside.

Using medium speed on mixer, cream butter. Add brown sugar gradually; mix until fluffy. Add eggs, one at a time, mixing well after each addition.

Sift together flour, salt, baking powder and spices. Using low speed, mix in half of flour mixture. Stir in last half by hand. Fold in pumpkin-soda mixture.

Drop by teaspoon on greased cookie sheet. Make shallow depression in center with back of spoon. Into this place ½ teaspoon of filling. Cover with additional dough. Sprinkle nut mixture on top, pressing into dough.

Bake at 350° for about 10 - 13 minutes or until almost no imprint remains when lightly touched with finger. Makes about 4 dozen filled or 6 dozen plain cookies.

Filling

Chop until fine and well-mixed: ½ cup candied orange peel, ½ cup candied red cherries or red or yellow candied pineapple, and ½ cup orange marmalade.

Topping

Mix together ½ cup finely chopped nuts, ½ cup sugar, 1 teaspoon cinnamon.

Note:
1. If desired, add 1 cup each raisins and/or nuts to dough before adding pumpkin mixture. Omit filling.
2. Omit topping and frost warm cookies with Orange Glaze. Sprinkle with chopped nuts.

Marilyn Martell
Thousand Oaks, California

Marilyn Martell, *County Fair Prize Cookies*, Prize Publishers, P. O. Box 281, Port Hueneme, California. Used by permission of Prize Publishers.

Brownie Drops

A brownie that everyone loves – even those who don't really care for chocolate! These tender cookies are made with German's Sweet Chocolate to give them a mild and marvelous milk chocolate flavor!

2 pkgs. German's Sweet Chocolate
1 tablespoon butter
2 eggs
¾ cup sugar
¼ cup flour, unsifted
¼ teaspoon baking powder
¼ teaspoon cinnamon
⅛ teaspoon salt
½ teaspoon vanilla
¾ cup finely chopped pecans

Melt chocolate and butter over hot water; cool.

Beat eggs until foamy, then add sugar, 2 tablespoons at a time, beating until thickened (5 minutes on electric mixer). Blend in chocolate.

Sift dry ingredients together; blend into chocolate mixture. Stir in vanilla and nuts.

Drop by teaspoons onto greased baking sheet.

Bake at 350° 8 to 10 minutes or until cookies feel "set" when very lightly touched. Makes about 3 dozen.

Joni Jensen
Provo, Utah

Chocolate Drop Cookies

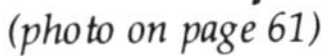
(photo on page 61)

A chocolate-lovers idea of a great cookie!

½ cup butter
1 cup sugar
1 egg
2 oz. unsweetened chocolate, melted and cooled
1/3 cup buttermilk
1 teaspoon vanilla
1¾ cups flour
½ teaspoon soda
½ teaspoon salt
1 cup chopped nuts
Chocolate Icing

Mix thoroughly butter, sugar, egg, chocolate, buttermilk and vanilla.

Sift flour, soda and salt together. Stir into butter mixture. Add nuts. Chill 1 hour.

Drop by rounded teaspoonsful 2-inches apart onto ungreased baking sheet.

Bake at 400° for 8 to 10 minutes. Immediately remove from baking sheet. Cool. Frost with Chocolate Icing.

Chocolate Icing

2 oz. unsweetened chocolate
2 tablespoons butter
3 tablespoons water
2 cups confectioners' sugar
Walnut halves

Melt chocolate and butter over low heat. Remove from heat, blend in water and confectioners' sugar. Decorate with a walnut half.

Mrs. Harold Mortensen
Raymond, Nebraska

Date Puffs

These tasty, tender meringue puffs are chock full of dates and nuts, and so satisfying when you crave a cookie that's different.

3 egg whites
1 cup sugar
2½ teaspoons cornstarch
⅛ teaspoon salt
1 lb. dates, finely chopped
1 cup chopped nuts
1 teaspoon vanilla

Combine egg whites, sugar, cornstarch and salt in top of double boiler. Place over hot water and beat until mixture will stand in peaks, about 7 minutes.

Remove from hot water and cool. Add dates, nuts and vanilla.

Drop by spoonfuls on slightly greased cookie sheet.

Bake at 325° for 12 to 15 minutes.

Doris Downs
Murray, Utah

California Carrot Cookies

Mrs. Huber adds coconut to her carrot cookies for extra flavor and texture then tops them with a creamy Orange Butter Icing. Delectable!

1 cup shortening
¾ cup sugar
1 cup carrots (cooked and mashed)
2 eggs
2 cups flour, sifted
2 teaspoons baking powder
½ teaspoon salt
¾ cup shredded coconut

Cream shortening, sugar, carrots and eggs thoroughly.

Sift dry ingredients together; stir into creamed mixture. Stir in coconut. Drop about 2 inches apart on lightly greased baking sheet.

Bake at 400° until no imprint remains when touched. Spread with orange butter icing when cool.

Orange Butter Icing

1/3 cup soft butter
3 cups sifted confectioners' sugar
3 teaspoons cream (approx.)
1 egg yolk (optional)
1½ teaspoons vanilla

Blend ingredients together until creamy and of spreading consistency.

Mrs. Virginia Huber
Tujunga, California

Coconut - Carrot Cookies

"A joy to make with it's whipped-cream-like batter," states Mrs. Strand, "and so refreshingly different!"

½ cup soft margarine
½ cup shortening
¾ cup sugar
2 eggs, beaten
1 cup mashed, cooked carrots
2 cups flour
2 teaspoons baking powder
¼ teaspoon salt
¾ cup flaked coconut

Cream margarine, shortening and sugar until light. Add beaten eggs; mix well. Blend in carrots.

Sift dry ingredients together and add to creamed mixture. Fold in coconut. Drop 2-inches apart on lightly greased baking sheet.

Bake at 350° for 10 to 12 minutes or until no imprint remains. Frost.

Orange Butter Frosting

1/3 cup soft margarine
2½ cups powdered sugar
2 - 3 tablespoons orange juice
1½ tablespoons grated rind

Cream margarine and powdered sugar until smooth. Add orange juice and orange rind; beat until of smooth spreading consistency.

Mrs. Phyliss A. Strand
St. Louis Park, Minnesota

Carrot-Oatmeal Cookies

Cookies that taste good and are good for you! So moist and delicious children will willingly pass up those empty-calorie snacks for these wholesome cookies.

2 cups whole wheat pastry flour, sifted
1 teaspoon baking powder
¼ teaspoon soda
½ teaspoon salt
¼ teaspoon nutmeg
¼ teaspoon cinnamon
1 cup rolled oats
1 cup raisins
½ cup margarine
1 cup brown sugar
2 eggs, beaten
1/3 cup milk
1½ cups grated raw carrots

Sift flour. Measure and sift again into large mixing bowl with baking powder, soda, salt and spices. Add rolled oats and raisins.

Cream margarine and sugar; add eggs, milk and carrots, blending well. Add to flour mixture, mixing well. Drop by teaspoons onto greased cookie sheet.

Bake 15 minutes at 350°. Makes 5 dozen.

Audrey Martinec
Orange County, California

Golden Carrot Cookies

Everyone loves Carrot Cake and they'll love Carrot Cookies, too! They're so moist and tender, and, they keep well.

¾ cup shortening
¾ cup sugar
1 egg
1 cup mashed, cooked carrots
3 teaspoons orange juice
2 cups flour
2 teaspoons baking powder
¼ teaspoon salt

Cream shortening and sugar until light. Add egg, carrots and orange juice, blending well.

Add sifted dry ingredients, mixing well. Drop from spoon onto greased cookie sheet.

Bake at 400° about 12 minutes. Frost while still hot.

Creamy Orange Frosting

1 cup powdered sugar
½ teaspoon grated orange peel
Orange Juice

Combine powdered sugar and orange peel. Add enough orange juice to make of spreading consistency.

Mrs. A. J. Smith
Phoenix, Arizona

Grandmother's Oatmeal Cookies

The old-fashioned flavor in these cookies is obtained by allowing the raisins to stand at room temperature in a vanilla-egg mixture.

3 eggs, well beaten
1 cup raisins
1 teaspoon vanilla
1 cup shortening (may be part butter)
1 cup brown sugar
1 cup granulated sugar
2½ cups flour
1 teaspoon salt
2 teaspoons soda
1 teaspoon cinnamon
2 cups oatmeal
½ cup chopped walnuts

Combine eggs, raisins, and vanilla; let stand 1 hour.

Cream shortening and sugars until very light and fluffy.

Sift flour, salt, soda and cinnamon into creamed mixture; mix well. Blend in egg mixture. Stir in oatmeal and walnuts. (Dough will be stiff). Drop by teaspoonful on ungreased cookie sheet or roll into small balls and flatten.

Bake at 350° for 10 to 20 minutes.

Barbara Cundall
Glendo, Wyoming

Chewy Coconut Macaroons

So easy – just mix, bake and enjoy!

1½ cups flaked coconut
1/3 cup sugar
⅛ teaspoon salt
2 tablespoons flour
2 egg whites
½ teaspoon almond extract

Combine coconut, sugar, salt and flour. Stir in egg whites and almond extract; mix well.

Drop by teaspoonful onto lightly greased cookie sheets.

Bake at 325° for 20 minutes or until golden brown around the edges. Remove from cookie sheets at once. Makes approximately 1½ dozen.

Donna M. Morgan
Albuquerque, New Mexico

Chocolate Coconut Macaroons

Mrs. Handley loves to cook, bake, and compete in local and national cooking contests. And, she's good at it, too – she has a goodly number of ribbons to prove it! She originally received this prize-winning recipe from her sister who also enjoys serving it as a special treat at Christmastime.

2 egg whites
¼ teaspoon salt
½ cup granulated sugar
½ teaspoon vanilla
1 6-oz. pkg. semi-sweet chocolate, melted
1½ cups shredded coconut

Beat egg whites until foamy; beat in salt. Sift sugar in gradually, beating well after each addition until mixture stands in peaks.

Fold in vanilla, cooled chocolate and coconut. Drop by teaspoonful on ungreased cookie sheet lined with brown paper.

Bake at 325° for 20 minutes. Cool before removing from cookie sheet.

Mrs. Katherine (Kay) Handley
Columbia Heights, Minnesota

Mardi Gras Macaroons

Marvelous, make-ahead macaroons! They stand for at least two hours so you can easily delight guests with warm-from-the-oven macaroons, even with a busy last minute entertaining schedule.

½ lb. almond paste
1 cup granulated sugar
3 egg whites
1/3 cup confectioners' sugar
¼ cup sifted cake flour
⅛ teaspoon salt

Cut almond paste into very small pieces. Gradually stir in granulated sugar and unbeaten egg whites and blend thoroughly.

Sift together confectioners' sugar, cake flour and salt; blend into almond paste mixture.

Drop by teaspoonsful onto cookie sheet covered with ungreased brown paper. Flatten slightly with finger dipped in cold water. Cover with waxed paper and let stand two hours or longer.

Bake at 300° for 30 minutes. Makes 2½ dozen.

Nancy Dworzak
Orange County, California

Coconut Oatmeal Cookies

The kind of cookie you like to find in the cookie jar.

1 cup margarine
1 cup granulated sugar
1 cup brown sugar, firmly packed
2 eggs
1 teaspoon vanilla
1-2/3 cups unsifted flour
1 teaspoon baking powder
½ teaspoon soda
½ teaspoon salt
1½ cups quick cooking oats
1 cup chopped nuts
2 cups shredded coconut

Cream margarine and sugars until fluffy. Beat in eggs and vanilla.

Sift flour, baking powder, soda and salt together. Blend into creamed mixture. Stir in rolled oats, nuts and coconut. Drop by rounded teaspoonfuls about 1½ inches apart on a greased baking sheet; press into flat rounds about ¼-inch thick with tines of fork.

Bake at 350° for 10 to 12 minutes or until lightly browned. Makes 8 dozen cookies.

Mrs. Ralph A. Ochs
Vallejo, California

Oatmeal Macaroons

A cookie jar favorite. They can also be made Paul Bunyan size by spooning by the tablespoon onto the cookie sheet.

1 cup shortening
1 cup brown sugar
1 cup granulated sugar
½ teaspoon vanilla
2 eggs
1¼ cups flour
1 teaspoon soda
½ teaspoon salt
2 teaspoons cinnamon
½ teaspoon nutmeg
1 cup raisins
3 cups rolled oats, uncooked, (quick or old-fashioned)

Cream shortening and sugar. Add eggs and vanilla; beat thoroughly.

Sift flour, soda, salt and spices into shortening mixture; blend well. Stir in raisins and oatmeal. Drop by teaspoonsful onto greased cookie sheets.

Bake at 350° for 12 minutes or until lightly browned. Makes 5½ dozen. For a larger cookie, drop the dough by tablespoons, spread slightly. Bake for about 14 to 15 minutes. Makes about 30.

Bernice A. Heuer
East Detroit, Michigan

Rolled cookies

Nutjammers

"My children manage to eat these cookies as fast as I can bake them!," comments Jamie Sanchez. That's not too surprising – the cookies are a delectable combination of cream cheese pastry and apricot or pineapple-almond filling. Delicious!

1 cup butter
1 8-oz. pkg. cream cheese
2 cups flour, sifted
½ teaspoon baking powder
2 cups finely chopped almonds
1 12-oz. jar apricot or pineapple jam
2 teaspoons granulated sugar
1/3 cup powdered sugar

Cream butter and cream cheese.

Sift flour and baking powder together; stir into creamed mixture.

Chill 2 - 3 hours. Divide dough into 4 equal parts. Work with ¼ of dough at a time, refrigerating the remaining dough.

Roll dough very thin (1/16th") on lightly floured board. Cut into 2-inch squares or use small diamond cookie cutter.

Combine almonds, jam and granulated sugar; place 1 teaspoon of mixture in center of square and top with another square. Press edges together with tines of fork.

Bake at 375° for 15 - 20 minutes or until lightly browned. When completely cool, sprinkle tops with confectioners' sugar. Makes about 5 dozen.

Jamie Sanchez
LeGrand, California

Apricot Cream Cheese Pastry Hearts

Tender, melt-in-your-mouth cream cheese pastries with a yummy apricot filling.

2 cups all-purpose flour
¼ teaspoon salt
1 cup butter
1 8-oz. package cream cheese
Apricot or raspberry preserves
2 eggs, beaten

Sift flour and salt into a medium sized bowl. Cut in butter and cream cheese with pastry blender or 2 knives. Shape into ball; wrap in waxed paper; chill.

Roll out ⅛-inch thick on floured surface. Cut out heart-shaped cookies with a 3-inch cutter. Arrange half the hearts on a lightly greased cookie sheet. In center of each, place 1 scant teaspoonful of preserves. Brush edges with egg; cover each with another cut-out heart. Press edges together with fork. Brush tops with beaten egg; sprinkle with granulated sugar, if desired.

Bake at 400° for 12 minutes, or until golden. Makes 2½ dozen.

Joni Jensen
Provo, Utah

St. James Spice Cookies

These spicy cookies won not only the Blue Ribbon but the Sweepstakes as well at the Minnesota State Fair!

2/3 cup shortening
1 cup sugar
1 egg
¼ cup molasses
2 cups flour
1 teaspoon soda
1 teaspoon salt
1 teaspoon cinnamon
1 teaspoon ginger
1 teaspoon cloves

Cream shortening and sugar. Add egg and molasses.

Sift dry ingredients together and mix into shortening mixture.

Chill dough slightly. Roll portions of dough ⅛-inch thick on floured board and cut with cookie cutter into desired shapes.

Bake at 350° for 8 to 10 minutes. Frost when cooled.

Creamy Frosting

1/3 cup soft butter
3 cups sifted powdered sugar
3 tablespoons cream
1½ teaspoons vanilla

Blend butter and powdered sugar together. Add cream and vanilla; stir until smooth.

Mrs. Dale Radenbaugh
St. James, Minnesota

Magic Cookies

Trudy Richardson's decorated sugar cookies are works of art! In fact, she has received top honors at a national cooking contest in competition with master chefs from famous restaurants all over the United States!

Her recipe for cookie dough is nothing unusual. The extra touch that makes her cookies so special is the edible glitter that she sprinkles on them for a dazzling sparkle! The glitter, Brilliantine, is so easy to make and can be done in any color desired to suit the holiday or special occasion.

1 cup sugar
2/3 cup butter or margarine
1 tablespoon white corn syrup
2 eggs or 4 egg yolks
1 teaspoon flavoring
2 teaspoons baking powder
1 teaspoon salt
2½ - 3 cups flour
Small amount of milk
Nuts, fruit peels, etc. as desired

Cream sugar and butter until light and fluffy. Add corn syrup; blend. Add eggs, one at a time, beating well after each addition. Stir in flavoring.

Stir baking powder and salt into first cup of flour. Add gradually to creamed mixture. Add remaining flour as needed to form soft dough.

Add a small amount of milk if necessary to keep dough of soft consistency — this will depend on whether additional dry ingredients such as cocoa are added. Add nuts, fruit peels, cocoa, crushed peppermint or other additions as desired.

Roll ⅜-inch thick on well-floured cloth. Cut into desired shapes; place on ungreased cookie sheets.

Bake at 375° for 6 to 8 minutes. Cool on paper towels. Sprinkle with Brilliantine, or frost then sprinkle with Brilliantine.

Brilliantine

2 tablespoons Gum Arabic
(Baker's supply or drug store)
1/3 - ½ cup water
Blue food color or color as desired

Combine Gum Arabic, water and a **very tiny** dot of blue food color, or desired color in saucepan. Cook over medium heat, stirring constantly, until Gum Arabic dissolves. Strain through cloth.

Brush on aluminum foil; place in 350° oven. Close oven door for 1 minute; open; turn off heat. Syrup will dry and crystals will form causing a crackling noise. Turn oven on occasionally to keep oven warm.

When crackling noise stops, shake glitter off foil. Sift through strainer for fine dust.

Trudy Richardson
Omaha, Nebraska

Deluxe Sugar Cookies

This sugar cookie has the flavor that is missing in most sugar cookies and is well-deserving of the Sweepstakes Rosette and the Archway Cookie Award for the best home-style cookie at the State Fair.

1 cup butter, softened
1½ cups confectioners' sugar
1 egg
1 teaspoon vanilla
½ teaspoon almond extract
2½ cups flour
1 teaspoon soda
1 teaspoon cream of tartar
Granulated sugar

Cream thoroughly the butter, confectioners' sugar, egg, vanilla and almond extract. Blend in flour, soda and cream of tartar.

Cover; chill 2 to 3 hours. Divide dough in half. Roll each half 3/16-inch thick on a lightly floured board. Cut into desired shapes, sprinkle with granulated sugar. Place on lightly greased baking sheet.

Bake at 375° for 7 to 8 minutes or until light brown on edges. Makes about 5 dozen.

Mrs. Cyril Bauer
Harrisonville, Missouri

Sour Cream Sugar Cookies

Sour cream gives these sugar cookies tenderness and a "Bake Shoppe" flavor.

4 cups flour
1 teaspoon baking powder
½ teaspoon baking soda
½ teaspoon salt
½ teaspoon nutmeg
1 cup butter
1½ cups sugar
1 egg
½ cup sour cream
1 teaspoon vanilla

Sift together flour, baking powder, baking soda, salt and nutmeg.

In a large bowl beat together butter, sugar, and egg. Mix in sour cream and vanilla until smooth. Gradually add flour mixture.

Divide dough into 4 parts, wrap in wax paper and refrigerate overnight. Roll dough to ¼-inch thickness and cut into desired shapes. Sprinkle with sugar.

Bake on greased cookie sheets for 10 to 12 minutes at 375°.

Jacque Larson
Phoenix, Arizona

Fancy Shortbread Cookies

A family favorite that is perfect for parties when cut into fancy shapes with tiny cookie cutters.

I cup butter
1 cup powdered sugar
1 teaspoon vanilla extract
½ teaspoon orange extract
2 cups flour
¼ cup cornstarch

Cream butter; add sugar slowly and beat until fluffy. Add flavorings.

Sift flour and cornstarch together; stir into butter mixture, mixing thoroughly.

Chill overnight. Roll out on floured board to 1/3-inch thickness. Cut with round or fancy cookie cutters.

Bake at 350° for 18 to 20 minutes on ungreased cookie sheets until very light tan in color. Cool on wire racks.

Bernice Glendening
Bakersfield, California

Honey Tea Cookies

The surprise ingredient in Mrs. Toth's tempting Tea Cookies is wheat germ! It gives these cookies a rich toasty flavor you'll love!

½ cup butter or margarine
½ cup honey
1¾ cups flour
1 teaspoon baking soda
½ teaspoon cinnamon
¼ teaspoon ground cloves
¼ teaspoon allspice
1/3 cup wheat germ

Cream butter and honey until light.

Sift together flour, soda, and spices; mix in wheat germ. Blend into creamed mixture.

Chill 1 hour.

Roll out on a lightly floured board to about ⅛-inch thick. Cut with floured cookie cutter. Place on greased cookie sheets.

Bake at 350° for 8 to 10 minutes. Cool. Spread with Honey Lemon Icing.

Honey Lemon Icing

¾ cup confectioners' sugar
1 tablespoon honey
1 tablespoon lemon juice

Blend confectioners' sugar with honey and enough lemon juice to make of spreading consistency. Beat until smooth.

Mrs. Steve Toth
West Allis, Wisconsin

Refrigerator cookies

Butterscotch Refrigerator Cookies

Barbara Cundall's cookies not only won the Blue Ribbon, but they were also included in the prize-winning selection of cookies presented to Wyoming's Governor, Ed Herschler.

1 cup soft butter or margarine
2 cups brown sugar
2 eggs
1 teaspoon vanilla
3½ cups flour
1 teaspoon soda
½ teaspoon salt
1 cup finely chopped nuts

Cream butter until light; gradually beat in sugar. Add eggs and vanilla; continue beating until very light and fluffy.

Sift dry ingredients together. Blend in half of flour mixture on low speed of mixer. Blend in remaining flour with hands, forming a stiff dough. Stir in nuts.

Turn dough out onto lightly floured surface. Divide in thirds. Shape each section of dough into a roll 8 inches long. Wrap in plastic; refrigerate until firm — 8 hours or overnight.

Cut into ⅛-inch slices; place 2-inches apart on ungreased cookie sheet.

Bake at 375° for 7 to 10 minutes or until lightly browned.

Note: Rolls may be stored in refrigerator a week or 10 days.

Barbara Cundall
Glendo, Wyoming

Maple-Nut Pinwheel Cookies

Rich, Vermont maple flavoring and walnuts combine for a tempting taste-treat.

½ cup butter
1 cup sugar
1 egg, beaten
1 teaspoon vanilla
1½ cups flour
¼ teaspoon salt
1½ teaspoons baking powder
½ cup finely chopped walnuts
1½ teaspoons Mapeline brand maple flavoring

Cream butter and sugar until light. Add egg, beat well. Mix in vanilla.

Sift dry ingredients together; stir into creamed mixture, mixing well.

Divide dough in half. To one-half the dough, add nuts. Add Mapeline (adjust amount to personal taste) to other half, mixing well.

Roll out between 2 sheets of waxed paper into oblong 1/8-inch thick. Chill 30 minutes.

Remove top layer of waxed paper from each section of dough. Place maple dough on top of nut dough. Remove sheet of wax paper from top.

Roll jelly-roll fashion into long roll. Wrap in waxed paper. Chill 12 to 24 hours. Slice 1/8" to 1/4" thick and place on greased cookie sheet.

Bake at 400° for 8 to 10 minutes. Makes about 40 cookies.

Mrs. Frances Ranch
Crescent City, California

Choco-Mint Sandwiches

These chocolate refrigerator cookies have a refreshing green mint filling that is surprisingly easy to make!

3/4 cup margarine
1 cup sugar
1 egg
1/2 teaspoon vanilla
2 cups flour
3/4 cup cocoa
1 teaspoon baking powder
1/2 teaspoon soda
1/2 teaspoon salt
1/4 cup milk
Mint filling:
3 tablespoons margarine
1 1/2 cups powdered sugar
1 tablespoon milk
Peppermint to taste
Green food coloring

Cream margarine and sugar. Add egg and vanilla, blend well.

Add flour, cocoa, baking powder, soda and salt, along with milk.

Shape into two 10 x 1 1/2-inch rolls. Chill.

Cut into 1/8-inch slices and place on ungreased cooky sheet.

Bake at 325° for 10 minutes. When cool, combine filling ingredients and fill cookies.

Vicki Green
Albuquerque, New Mexico

Chocolate Pinwheels

Besides being a wife, mother, and prize-winning cookie-maker, Julie Cademarti has found time to be a television studio engineer, Senior Clerk for the California Department of Justice, a student of broadcasting at California State University, and a freelance writer! Her Chocolate Pinwheels are a favorite with the Cademarti family – especially with her husband, Ben, a deputy sheriff of Placer County.

¾ cup shortening (part butter or margarine)
1 cup sugar
2 eggs
1 teaspoon vanilla
2½ cups flour
1 teaspoon baking powder
1 teaspoon salt
2 squares unsweetened chocolate, melted

Cream shortening and sugar. Add eggs and vanilla; mix thoroughly.

Stir flour, baking powder and salt together and blend into shortening mixture.

Divide dough in half. Blend the melted and cooled chocolate into one half. Chill dough.

Roll remaining dough into an oblong, 12 x 9-inches. Roll chocolate dough same size; lay on top of white. Roll layers of dough together until 3/16-inch thick. Roll up tightly, beginning at wide side.

Chill again.

Cut into ⅛-inch thick slices; place on ungreased cooky sheet.

Bake at 400° for 8 to 10 minutes. Makes 7 dozen cookies.

Cathy Cademarti
Roseville, California

Coconut-Oatmeal Crisps

Joni Jensen began winning Blue Ribbons and Sweepstakes Awards at the age of 12! Besides competing successfully in adult cooking competitions at the age of 16 she has also received awards for her knitting and sewing. She's a very talented teenager!

1 cup cake flour
½ teaspoon soda
¼ teaspoon salt
2 cups oatmeal
1 cup flaked coconut
½ cup shortening
1 cup sugar
1 egg
¼ cup evaporated milk
1 teaspoon vanilla

Sift dry ingredients together. Add oatmeal and coconut; set aside.

Cream shortening and sugar until light. Add egg and beat well. Combine milk and vanilla.

Add dry ingredients to creamed mixture alternately with milk and vanilla mixture, blending thoroughly.

Form into rolls, wrap in waxed paper and chill overnight in refrigerator.

Slice 1/8-inch thick and place on greased cookie sheet.

Bake at 400° for 12 minutes or until light golden brown. Makes about 7 dozen cookies.

Joni Jensen
Provo, Utah

Tropical Fruit-Filled Cookies

This winning recipe won the Sweepstakes Rosette, the "Best of Cook," and the Archway Cookie Award!

1 cup margarine
1 cup granulated sugar
1 cup brown sugar
3 eggs, well beaten
4 cups flour
1/4 teaspoon salt
1/2 teaspoon soda
1 teaspoon vanilla

Cream shortening; add sugar gradually. Add eggs and mix well. Sift together dry ingredients and add to first mixture. Blend thoroughly.

Divide dough into two parts and chill thoroughly for easier handling. Divide each ball into halves. Roll each section on floured wax paper and spread with date-filling mixture. Roll up jelly-roll fashion. Place in freezer until it will slice nicely. Slice 1/4 inch thick.

Bake at 375° for 12 minutes.

Tropical Filling

2 1/4 cups chopped dates
1/4 cup crushed pineapple
1 cup sugar
1 cup water
1/2 cup finely chopped nuts

Combine all the ingredients and cook over low heat until thick. Cool.

Josephine Smith
Wichita, Kansas

Date Pinwheels

"These are not the easiest cookies to make," states Mrs. Smith, "but they are my favorite."

1 lb. pitted dates, cut up
½ cup water
½ cup sugar
2 cups sifted flour
½ teaspoon baking soda
½ teaspoon salt
½ cup butter or margarine
½ cup brown sugar
½ cup granulated sugar
1 egg, beaten
½ teaspoon vanilla
1 cup finely chopped nuts

Combine dates, water and sugar in saucepan; cook until thick, stirring constantly. Cool.

Sift flour, soda, and salt together; set aside.

Cream butter, blend in sugars. Add egg and beat until light and fluffy. Stir in vanilla. Stir in flour mixture and quickly work dough until smooth.

Chill thoroughly.

Divide dough into 2 parts. Place one part on lightly floured board. Roll in rectangle ¼-inch thick.

Combine date mixture and nuts. Spread half the mixture evenly over dough. Roll up and wrap in wax paper. Repeat with other half of dough and date mix. Chill until firm.

Cut in ¼-inch slices. Place on greased cookie sheets.

Bake at 400° 8 to 10 minutes. Remove from pans at once.

Mrs. A. J. Smith
Phoenix, Arizona

Double Pecan Cookies

Party-pretty pecan cookies that are "just right" for almost any occasion.

¾ cup shortening
1½ cups brown sugar
1 egg
2 cups flour, sifted
½ teaspoon salt
⅛ teaspoon soda
¼ cup chopped pecans
¼ cup whole pecans

Cream shortening and sugar until light and fluffy. Blend in eggs.

Sift dry ingredients 3 times; add to shortening mixture. Stir in chopped nuts.

Shape into 1" diameter rolls. Wrap in waxed paper and chill. Slice thin (1/8" thick); place on lightly greased cookie sheet. Top with pecan halves. Bake at 350° for 8 to 10 minutes.

Mrs. Jim (Marilyn) Delleney
Albuquerque, New Mexico

Date Crinkles

Joanne Wacek added butter and almond flavorings to her cookies to give them a richer flavor that the judges loved – they awarded her date pinwheel cookies the Blue Ribbon.

1 cup shortening
1 cup granulated sugar
1 cup brown sugar
1 teaspoon butter flavoring
2 eggs, well beaten
1 teaspoon vanilla
½ teaspoon almond extract
1½ cups flour, sifted
1 teaspoon salt
1 teaspoon soda
3 cups quick oatmeal, uncooked
1 cup chopped pecans

Cream shortening, sugars and butter flavoring until fluffy. Add beaten eggs, vanilla and almond extract; beat well.

Sift flour, salt and soda together; add to creamed mixture. Stir in oatmeal and pecans; mix well.

Divide dough in half. On lightly oiled wax paper 24-inches long, pat half the dough with a lightly oiled wooden spoon until dough is about ¼-inch thick and 5-inches wide. Spread half the filling **smoothly** over the dough.

Roll, jelly-roll fashion to about 1½-inches in diameter. Wrap in wax paper. Repeat with second half of dough and filling.

Chill in freezer 30 to 40 minutes or refrigerate overnight. Slice ¼-inch thick and place on ungreased cookie sheets.

Bake at 350° for 8 to 12 minutes or until golden brown. Makes 3½ dozen.

Date Filling

1½ cups dates, chopped
1/3 cup sugar
1/3 cup water

Combine ingredients in saucepan. Cook over medium heat until thick, stirring constantly (about 3 - 4 minutes). Set aside to cool.

Joanne Wacek
Albuquerque, New Mexico

Coconut Dreams

An Archway Cookie Award winner at the Minnesota State Fair.

1 cup butter
½ cup sugar
2 cups unsifted flour
1 3½-oz. can flaked coconut

Cream butter and sugar until fluffy. Add flour, ½ cup at a time, beating well after each addition. Fold in coconut.

Form into 2 rolls, 2½-inches thick and 6 inches long, on waxed paper. Wrap in waxed paper; refrigerate overnight.

Slice rolls ¼-inch thick and place on ungreased teflon cookie sheets.

Bake at 300° for 25 minutes or until coconut is slightly toasted. (Watch carefully during the last few minutes of baking so coconut doesn't burn).

Mrs. Lois Ellerbusch
Fredley, Minnesota

Mother's Orange Almond-Icebox Cookies

Doubly-good and doubly-flavored with orange – orange juice and orange rind give these cookies their sunny orange flavor.

1 cup soft butter
½ cup sugar
½ cup brown sugar
1 egg
2 tablespoons orange juice
2¼ cups flour
½ teaspoon salt
½ teaspoon soda
1 tablespoon grated orange rind
½ cup blanched almonds, chopped
¼ cup flour

Cream butter thoroughly and gradually add sugar. Add brown sugar and cream well. Add egg, beat well. Add orange juice.

Sift together 2¼ cups flour, salt, soda; add to first mixture, beating well.

Coat the orange rind and blanched almonds with the ¼ cup flour. Add to butter mixture. Mix dough well.

Form into a roll, wrap in wax paper and chill for at least 3 hours. Dough keeps well in the refrigerator for several days.

When ready to bake, cut in thin slices and bake on cooky sheets in a hot oven (400°) for about 8 minutes. Do not let them get too brown.

Mary Mason Campbell
Orange County, California

Carmel Nut Cookies

A Sweepstakes-winning recipe from a winner of over 300 Blue Ribbons!

1 cup shortening, part butter
2 cups brown sugar, packed
2 eggs
3½ cups flour, sifted
½ teaspoon salt
1 teaspoon soda
1 cup finely chopped nuts

Cream shortening, sugar and eggs until light and fluffy.

Sift dry ingredients together; blend into creamed mixture. Stir in nuts.

Shape into 2 rolls 2-inches in diameter. Chill for 2 hours. Slice dough ⅛-inch thick and place on ungreased cookie sheet.

Bake at 400° for 8 to 10 minutes. Makes 12 dozen.

Shirley Crom
Smartville, California

Ginger Almond Cookies

So spicy and so good. Serve with tall glasses of cold milk for one great snack!

1½ cups butter
1½ cups granulated sugar
¾ cup honey
4 cups flour, unsifted
1½ teaspoons soda
1½ teaspoons salt
4 teaspoons ginger
1 tablespoon cinnamon
1 tablespoon cloves
1½ cups almonds, finely chopped

Cream butter and sugar until fluffy. Add honey in a fine stream.

Mix dry ingredients; stir into creamed mixture. Add almonds.

Shape in two thick rolls, each 2-inches in diameter. Wrap in waxed paper; refrigerate several hours until very firm. Cut cookies in ¼-inch slices.

Bake on lightly greased baking sheet at 350° for 12 to 15 minutes. Makes about 7½ dozen cookies.

Mrs. Randall Kirschman
La Canada, California

Pressed cookies

Spritz Cookies

A simple but special cookie recipe from the winner of the Champion Baker Plaque at the Sandwich, Illinois County Fair and the Archway Best Cookie Award.

2 cups butter or margarine
2 cups sugar
2 egg yolks
4 cups flour
1 teaspoon baking powder
Lemon extract

Cream butter and sugar; add egg yolks.

Blend in flour and baking powder. Add a drop or two of lemon extract. Mix well.

Put through cookie press.

Bake for 15 minutes at 325°. Makes about 100 cookies.

Mrs. Cyril Bauer
Harrisonville, Missouri

Almond Spritz

This butter-rich cookie not only won a Blue Ribbon, but was chosen as "Best of the Show."

1 cup butter
¾ cup sugar
1 egg
2¼ cups flour, sifted
½ teaspoon baking powder
Dash of salt
1 teaspoon almond extract

Cream butter and sugar until light and fluffy. Add egg; beat well.

Sift flour, baking powder and salt together; gradually blend into creamed mixture. Stir in almond flavoring.

Fill cookie press. Using star attachment, or any shape desired, space 1½-inches apart on lightly greased cookie sheet.

Bake at 350° 10 to 12 minutes, or until just slightly brown.

Myrla Allgier
Salt Lake City, Utah

Prize Peanut Butter Pillows

An unusual peanut butter cookie that has won an unusual amount of Blue Ribbons. No wonder, for these peanut butter cookies even have a peanut butter filling!

2 cups flour
1 teaspoon baking soda
¼ teaspoon salt
1 cup soft butter
1 cup light brown sugar
1 egg
1 cup creamy style peanut butter
1 teaspoon vanilla
Peanut Butter Filling:
½ cup crunchy peanut butter
2 tablespoons butter
¼ cup sugar

Measure flour, soda and salt into a sifter; set aside.

In large bowl, beat butter and sugar with electric mixer until light. Beat in egg, peanut butter and vanilla.

Sift half the flour mixture into butter mixture, blending at low speed of electric mixer. Stir in rest of flour mixture by hand. Refrigerate 30 minutes.

Make filling by blending ingredients.

Pack small amount of dough into cookie press. Using sawtooth disc, press 2″ lengths of dough 1″ apart on buttered cookie sheet. Top each with ½ teaspoon of filling. Cover completely with another pressed cooky. Press gently around edges. Sprinkle with granulated sugar.

Bake at 350° for 10 minutes. Cut between cookies. Remove to wire rack. Cool.

Variations: (All Blue Ribbon winners)

1. Use star cookie disc or other patterns. Decorate with melted chocolate chips and nuts.
2. Make filled cookies from round cut-outs using same filling. Seal edges with fork. Brush with egg yolk and 2 teaspoons water.
3. Make pinwheel (roll jellyroll fashion) or ribbon layered cookies using melted and cooled semi-sweet chocolate chips and rolled dough. Chill and slice with thin sharp knife. Watch baking time.
4. Make familiar crisscrosses with balls of dough.

Marilyn Martell
Thousand Oaks, California

Marilyn Martell, *County Fair Prize Cookies*, Prize Publishers, P. O. Box 281, Port Hueneme, California. Used by permission of Prize Publishers.

Shaped cookies

Good 'N Rich Cookies

This recipe not only received a Blue Ribbon and the Sweepstakes award, but it was also awarded a $1,000 bond from the Archway Company.

½ cup butter
½ cup oil
½ cup powdered sugar
½ cup granulated sugar
Grated rind of 1 lemon
1 egg yolk

2 cups flour
½ teaspoon soda
½ teaspoon cream of tartar
½ teaspoon salt
Almond or vanilla flavoring

Combine ingredients in first column; beat well with electric mixer.

Sift dry ingredients together; stir into creamed mixture. Add flavoring to taste; blend well.

Form into small balls and place ½-inch apart on cookie sheet. Using a spring form wire wisk, press down on each cookie to flatten and make a fancy design.

Bake at 350° for 15 minutes or until golden.

Mrs. Roy Johnson
Lindstrom, Minnesota

Walnut Party Puffs

"These are my fireman husband's favorite cookie!," states Meralee Light.

½ cup margarine
¼ cup sugar
Pinch of salt
1 teaspoon vanilla

1 cup finely chopped walnuts
1 cup flour, sifted
24 walnut halves

Cream margarine, sugar, salt and vanilla until very light and fluffy. Blend in nuts and flour until just mixed.

Chill dough for 1 hour. Form dough into 24 small balls, press walnut half into each.

Bake at 350° for 20 minutes on ungreased cookie sheet, or until lightly browned.

Meralee Light
Tracy, California

Pink Meringue Clouds

A tender peppermint-studded meringue tops these special cookies that will brighten the Christmas holidays or any special occasion.

Besides an interest in creative cooking, Bruce Jensen has an avid interest in World War II. He's read and re-read dozens of books on World War II and is virtually a walking encyclopedia of facts on armaments and battle strategy!

Cookie dough:

2 egg yolks
2½ cups flour
1 teaspoon salt
½ teaspoon baking powder
¾ cup sugar
2/3 cup shortening
¼ cup milk
1 teaspoon vanilla extract

Peppermint Meringue:

2 egg whites
¼ teaspoon salt
½ cup sugar
½ teaspoon vanilla extract
½ teaspoon vinegar
1 cup semi-sweet chocolate chips
1 cup coarsely crushed peppermint stick candy

In large mixer bowl combine cookie dough ingredients. Blend well with mixer. Chill while preparing meringue.

Prepare Peppermint Meringue by beating egg whites in small mixer bowl with salt until soft mounds form. Gradually add sugar; continue beating until stiff peaks form. Fold in vanilla extract, vinegar, chocolate chips and peppermint stick candy.

Shape dough into balls using a rounded teaspoon for each. Place on ungreased cookie sheets. Flatten with bottom of glass dipped in sugar.

Top each cookie with a rounded teaspoon of meringue.

Bake at 325° for 20 to 25 minutes. Makes 42 to 48 cookies.

Bruce Jensen
Provo, Utah

Butter-Nut Cookies

These buttery cookies look like miniature snowballs and are so attractive and appealing on a Christmas cookie tray.

1 cup butter
1 egg white, unbeaten
1/3 cup powdered sugar or
4 tablespoons sugar
1½ teaspoons vanilla
2½ cups flour
½ teaspoon salt
½ to 1 cup finely chopped pecans

Cream butter, egg white, sugar and vanilla until smooth. Add sifted flour, salt and nuts.

Roll into small balls or shape as desired.

Bake at 400° 10 to 12 minutes. Roll in confectioners's sugar while warm. Makes about 40 cookies.

Genevieve Palmer
Salt Lake City, Utah

Butter Balls

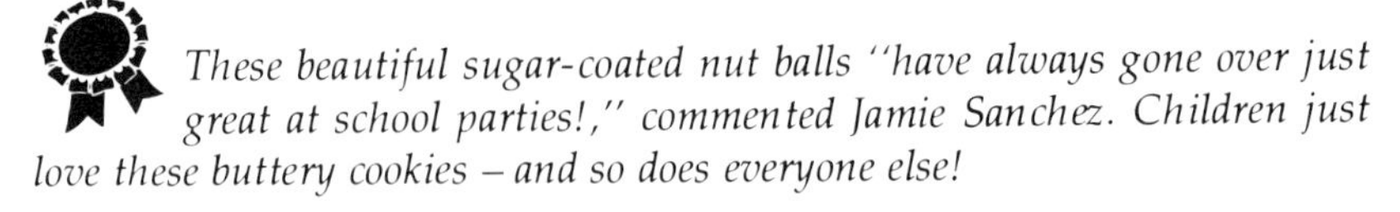

These beautiful sugar-coated nut balls "have always gone over just great at school parties!," commented Jamie Sanchez. Children just love these buttery cookies – and so does everyone else!

1 cup butter
½ cup confectioners' sugar
½ teaspoon vanilla
1¾ cups flour, sifted
½ cup chopped nuts
Confectioners' sugar

Cream butter and sugar until light and fluffy. Blend in vanilla and flour; stir in nuts.

Chill several hours for ease in handling. Shape into balls 1-inch in diameter; place on baking sheet.

Bake at 350° for 20 minutes. Roll balls while warm in confectioners' sugar. Place on wire rack to cool. Yield: 3 dozen.

Jamie Sanchez
LeGrand, California

Apricot Blossoms

(photo on cover)

"I'm not a cookie baker, I'm really a candle-maker," says Margaret Born. She's received ribbons in candle-making at national conventions, so she's a pretty fair candle-maker and cookie-maker. Mrs. Born received the biggest cookie prize at the Wisconsin State Fair – The Archway Sweepstakes Cookie Award and a check for $100 that was presented by singer Mac Davis. Quite an accomplishment – there were 85 entries!

1⅛ cups flour
1 teaspoon baking powder
Dash of salt
1/3 cup butter
½ cup sugar
1 egg, separated
1 tablespoon half and half
1 teaspoon vanilla
1/3 cup apricot preserves

Sift together flour, baking powder and salt; set aside.

Cream butter, sugar, egg yolk, half and half and vanilla. Blend dry ingredients into creamed mixture gradually; mix thoroughly.

Shape dough into balls, using a heaping tablespoon for each cookie. Place on lightly greased or nonstick cookie sheet; flatten slightly; brush with unbeaten egg white.

Bake at 350° for 12 minutes. Remove from oven; top each cookie with ½ teaspoon apricot preserves. Bake 3 minutes more. Makes about 1 dozen.

Margaret Born
Milwaukee, Wisconsin

Amish Sugar Cookies

These delicious cookies have won Blue Ribbons in state and county fairs in Kansas and Nebraska!

1 cup granulated sugar
1 cup confectioners' sugar
1 cup margarine
1 cup oil
2 eggs
1 teaspoon baking soda
1 teaspoon cream of tartar
½ teaspoon salt
1 teaspoon vanilla
4½ cups flour
Granulated sugar

Combine sugars, margarine, oil and eggs; beat well. Add remaining ingredients; mix well.

Refrigerate dough till chilled. Roll in balls; dip in granulated sugar. Place on cookie sheet; flatten with the bottom of a glass.

Bake at 375° for 10 to 12 minutes.

Darlene Tussing
Lincoln, Nebraska

Coconut Islanders

The Danish have a way with cookies – all their cookies are delectable, and this one is no exception!

1 cup flour
2 tablespoons cornstarch
½ cup confectioners' sugar
1 cup margarine
1½ cups coconut

Mix flour, cornstarch and sugar in small bowl. Blend in margarine to form a soft dough. Cover and chill.

Shape into small balls, about ¾-inch in diameter. Roll in coconut and place on ungreased baking sheets about 1½-inches apart. Flatten with lightly floured fork.

Bake at 300° for 20 to 25 minutes or until lightly browned.

Marie Laursen
Fortuna, California

Chocolate Crackles

Crunchy chocolate cookies that won the Archway Sweepstakes Award. They were a favorite with the judges and they're the McManus' favorite cookie. Besides tasting great, they're so easy to make and can even be made ahead of time and kept in the refrigerator for several days.

½ cup vegetable oil
4 squares chocolate, melted
2 cups sugar
4 eggs
2 teaspoons vanilla
2 cups flour
2 teaspoons baking powder
½ teaspoon salt
1 cup powdered sugar

Combine oil, melted chocolate and granulated sugar. Blend in eggs, one at a time, beating well after each addition. Add vanilla.

Sift flour, baking powder and salt together; blend into creamed mixture. Chill several hours or overnight.

Form into small balls and roll in powdered sugar. Place on greased baking sheet.

Bake at 350° for 12 - 15 minutes.

Clarice McManus
Huron, South Dakota

Chocolate Pixies

This recipe makes a **very** *large batch of cookies – 7 dozen! But, even that large amount is of no concern as these cookies are so good there just won't be any left!*

½ cup butter or margarine
4 oz. unsweetened chocolate
4 eggs
2 cups sugar
3 cups flour
1½ teaspoons baking powder
½ teaspoon salt
½ cup chopped walnuts
Powdered sugar

Melt butter and chocolate over low heat; cool.

Beat eggs and sugar until light. Gradually add chocolate mixture.

Sift dry ingredients together; gradually add to egg mixture. Stir in walnuts.

Chill dough at least 30 minutes. Shape into 1" diameter balls; roll in powdered sugar.

Bake at 350° for 15 to 18 minutes on lightly greased cookie sheet.

Mrs. Jim (Marilyn) Delleney
Albuquerque, New Mexico

Double Chocolate Crinkles

A prize-winning cookie from a prize-winning cook. Marilyn Martell's cookies have won the Sweepstakes awards at the Ventura County Fair and California State Fair several times!

1 cup oil
4 squares (4 oz.) unsweetened chocolate, melted
2 cups sugar
4 eggs
2 teaspoons vanilla
2 cups flour
2 teaspoons baking powder
½ teaspoon salt
1 6-oz. pkg. semi-sweet chocolate chips
1 cup sifted confectioners' sugar

Mix oil, chocolate and sugar. Blend in eggs, one at a time, until well mixed. Add vanilla.

Sift flour, baking powder and salt into oil mixture. Add chocolate chips.

Chill several hours or overnight.

Roll into balls 1″ in diameter and roll in confectioners' sugar. Place 2″ apart on oiled cookie sheet.

Bake at 350° for 10 minutes. Don't overbake. Remove hot cookies to rack. Makes 6 dozen.

Marilyn Martell
Thousand Oaks, California

Marilyn Martell, *County Fair Prize Cookies*, Prize Publishers, P. O. Box 281, Port Hueneme, California. Used by permission of Prize Publishers.

Molasses Crinkles

These spicy molasses cookies have chocolate chips as a surprise ingredient. They were good enough to help Mrs. Edgman win the Sweepstakes in cookie-making in the senior division while her daughter won the Sweepstakes in the junior division at the Tennessee State Fair. Talented family!

1 cup shortening
1 cup brown sugar
1 egg
¼ cup dark molasses
¼ cup milk
2½ cups flour
2 teaspoons soda
½ teaspoon ground cloves
1 teaspoon cinnamon
1 teaspoon ginger
1 6-oz. pkg. chocolate chips
Granulated sugar

Cream shortening, brown sugar, egg, molasses and milk until light.

Sift dry ingredients together and blend into shortening mixture. Fold in chocolate chips. Chill dough.

Roll into walnut-sized balls. Dip into granulated sugar.

Bake at 375° for 10 minutes.

Mrs. Jack (Elizabeth) Edgman
McEwen, Tennessee

Delicious - Fella's Love -
Glenn Says - tastes like Corey's

Sugar and Spice Cookies

Jack Korvink's favorite cookie! It was one of the judges favorites, too!

¾ cup shortening
1 cup brown sugar
¼ cup molasses
1 egg
2¼ cups flour, sifted
2 teaspoons soda
½ teaspoon salt
1 teaspoon ginger heaping
1 teaspoon cinnamon
½ teaspoon cloves

Cream shortening and brown sugar until light. Add molasses and egg; beat until fluffy.

Sift dry ingredients together; blend into creamed mixture, mixing well.

not necessary —Chill 1 hour. Form into small balls; roll into granulated sugar. Place 2-inches apart on cookie sheets. Rasin in center.

Bake at 375° about 10 minutes. Cool slightly, remove from cookie sheet.

Lila L. Korvink
Sacramento, California

Rum Chewy Cookies

Lillian Novak entered the Minnesota State Fair competition only once and came away with a Blue Ribbon for her Rum Chewy Cookies!

1 cup rolled oats
1 cup raisins
1 cup nuts
2 cups sugar
1 cup butter
2¼ cups flour
2 eggs
2 teaspoons soda
¼ teaspoon salt
1 teaspoon rum extract
Granulated sugar

Grind rolled oats, raisins and nuts through a food chopper.

Cream butter and sugar. Add the eggs, flour, soda, salt, rum extract, and the ground ingredients. Chill.

Roll into small balls about 1 teaspoon in size. Dip in sugar.

Bake at 350° for approximately 8 minutes. Yields 8 dozen.

Lillian Novak
New Prague, Minnesota

Pearl's Spice Cookies

Mrs. Cademarti has been winning prizes with this recipe since she was a teenager. She was given the recipe by Pearl Birkland, a winner of many recipe contests who originated this recipe.

¾ cup butter
1 cup sugar
4 tablespoons molasses
1 egg
2 cups flour
2 teaspoons soda
1 teaspoon cinnamon
1 teaspoon cloves
1 teaspoon ginger
Granulated sugar

Cream butter and sugar. Beat in molasses. Add egg and beat well.

Sift flour, baking soda and spices together; stir into butter mixture. (It's not necessary, but I chill the dough slightly before handling in this next step).

Shape dough into balls about the size of small walnuts and roll tops in granulated sugar. Place on ungreased cookie sheet.

Bake in preheated 375° oven for 8 to 10 minutes. Remove immediately from cookie sheet and place on cooling rack.

Makes 4 dozen.

Note: This cookie keeps and travels well. I've sent them across country on trips, and at Christmas they arrive in perfect condition and fresh.

Cathy Cademarti
Roseville, California

Anise Cookie Sticks

A prize-winning recipe from a great cook that has been winning Blue Ribbons and Sweepstakes awards for forty-three years!

¾ cup butter
1 cup sugar
4 eggs
3 cups flour
3 teaspoons baking powder
½ teaspoon salt
1 teaspoon anise seed
1 cup chopped nuts
Milk
Granulated sugar

Cream butter and sugar until light. Add eggs, one at a time, beating well after each addition. Continue beating until very light and fluffy.

Sift flour, baking powder, salt and anise seed together; mix into creamed mixture. Stir in nuts.

Divide dough into fourths. Place on greased cookie sheet; form into 4 rolls 1½-inches wide and the length of the baking sheet.

Bake at 350° for 30 to 35 minutes. Remove from oven. Cut diagonally into ¾-inch slices. Place cut side down on cookie sheets; brush with milk and sprinkle with granulated sugar.

Return to oven; bake 10 minutes longer until toasted and crisp.

Mrs. Louis Kekry
Crescent City, California